TRAVEL THERAPY

TRAVEL THERAPY

Where Do You Need To Go?

KAREN SCHALER

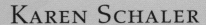

SEAL PRESS

Travel Therapy™
Where Do You Need to Go?

Copyright © 2009 by Karen Schaler

Front cover strip credits: Virgin Gorda, British Virgin Islands © Karen Schaler; Overwater Bungalow at Le Meridien Bora Bora, French Polynesia, Le Meridien Bora Bora © Tim-Mckenna.com; Alvadora Spa at Royal Palms Resort & Spa, Phoenix, Arizona © Royal Palms Resort & Spa; Turtle at Le Meridien Bora Bora, French Polynesia © Le Meridien Bora Bora, French Polynesia

Main photo: Jumby Bay, A Rosewood Resort, off Antigua, West Indies © Jumby Bay, A Rosewood Resort, off Antigua, West Indies

Back cover strip credits: The Regent Palms Turks and Caicos © The Regent Palm Turks and Caicos; South Africa Safari in Kruger National Park © Karen Schaler; The Centre of Well-Being, The Phoenician, Scottsdale, Arizona © The Phoenician; Children in Malawi, Africa © Karen Schaler.

Ambassadors for Children credo has been reprinted with the permission of the organization Ambassadors for Children. http://ambassadorsforchildren.org

Published by
Seal Press
A Member of Perseus Books Group
1700 Fourth Street
Berkeley, California

Library of Congress Cataloging-in-Publication Data

Schaler, Karen.
   Travel therapy : where do you need to go? / Karen Schaler.
      p. cm.
   ISBN-13: 978-1-58005-269-6
   ISBN-10: 1-58005-269-X
   1. Travel–Miscellanea. 2. Travel–Psychological aspects. 3.
Travel–Health aspects. I. Title.
   G151.S33 2008
   910.01'9–dc22
                                    2008039410

Cover design by Susan Koski Zucker
Interior design by Megan Cooney
Printed in the United States of America by R. R. Donnelley
Distributed by Publishers Group West

Travel Therapy, the name and brand, is the trademarked property of Karen Schaler, the *Travel Therapy* copyright owner.

To Mom
For letting me go when I needed to fly and always being there when I got lost . . .

To Kathy
For helping me find my way

To Dad
For changing the direction of the journey

Contents

"One's destination is never a place, but a new way of seeing things."

—HENRY MILLER

INTRODUCTION

*A*re you stressed out? Tired of your job? Bored with your relationship? Healing from an illness? Feeling uninspired or dealing with a loss? Pack your bags because *Travel Therapy* can help you find your way. Instead of sinking into depression after a heart-wrenching breakup or a botched business deal, or snapping at friends and family because you're stressed to the limit, now there's help. You can change your attitude by changing your environment. You've heard the phrase "you can't run away from your problems"—but you can embrace what's bothering you and use travel to help deal with whatever life throws your way.

Travel Therapy helps you pick the right vacation depending on what you're going through in life. If you're looking for an adventure, a romantic escape, a way to reconnect with your kids, a girlfriend getaway, a volunteer vacation, or just a blissed-out spa trip, *Travel Therapy* has you covered.

Where you go depends on how you want to feel. Inspired? Try heading to the mountains or a secluded beach. Empowered? Learn to drive a racecar, dive with sharks, or make chocolate. Energized? How about a spa, bike trip, or hike? The options are endless and the payback is priceless. So what are you waiting for? Pick the trip that fits you best and let *Travel Therapy* take you on one journey you can't afford to miss.

"Take two vacations, then call me in the morning."

—KAREN SCHALER

◀ *Beach bed on Virgin Gorda in the British Virgin Islands*
© KAREN SCHALER

"A journey of a thousand miles must begin with a single step."

—Lao Tzu

Chapter 1

Heartbreak Hotel

*B*reakups can either annihilate you or empower you—it's your choice. Of course, it helps if you pry your sticky fingers away from your double fudge ice cream carton and get off the couch and actually *do* something besides wallowing in self-pity. The key word here is move—and don't stop moving till you find yourself in a better frame of mind. Let's face it, breakups are gut-wrenching. Even when you're the one who ended things, it still stings.

After the initial breakup, when the shock wears off and you're ready to face the land of the living again, there are three surefire TRAVEL THERAPY ways to help you move on:

- Push Yourself Forward—Daring Destinations
- Sweat It Out of Your System—Action Adventures
- Lick Your Wounds and Heal—Soothing Spa Escapes

Which one is right for you? Take the TRAVEL THERAPY quiz to help you find your way.

◀ *The Centre for Well-Being Mediation Atrium, The Phoenician, Scottsdale, Arizona*
© THE PHOENICIAN, SCOTTSDALE, ARIZONA

TRAVEL THERAPY QUIZ

1. Right now are you in the mood to:
   a. Do something crazy
   b. Run a race
   c. Take a nap

2. If you're on a beach vacation you're most likely to be:
   a. Deep-sea diving
   b. Jogging on the sand
   c. Drinking a smoothie on the beach

3. With your breakup you are:
   a. Crying on and off
   b. Waterworks all the time
   c. All cried out

4. Your activity of choice is:
   a. Skydiving
   b. Biking
   c. Yoga

5. Your idea of a fun Saturday afternoon is:
   a. Extreme mountain biking
   b. Hiking with friends
   c. Curling up with a great book

6. Which animal would you rather be?
   a. Shark
   b. Monkey
   c. Fish

7. What is your preferred drink?
   a. Margaritas
   b. Sports drink
   c. Tea

8. Vehicle of choice?
   a. Racecar
   b. 4-wheel drive
   c. Luxury sedan

9. Your idea of a perfect date is:
   a. Tandem skydiving
   b. Hiking
   c. Dinner

10. Best buy?
    a. Life insurance
    b. Athletic gear
    c. Spa products

TRAVEL THERAPY DIAGNOSIS

If you chose mostly "A" answers, you need TRAVEL THERAPY that falls under Push Yourself Forward, where you are challenged both physically and mentally. In this category, you're literally pushed—if not shoved—out of your comfort level and right into some daring adventures.

If you answered mostly "B," then you need physical activity, so your best TRAVEL THERAPY options are adventure vacations, falling under Sweat It Out of Your System. In this category, you'll be so busy exerting yourself that you won't have time to wail about what went wrong in your relationship.

If you find you have mostly "C" answers, pick a trip under Lick Your Wounds and Heal. This TRAVEL THERAPY allows you to check your worries at the door and relax your mind, body, and spirit. A word of warning, though: For this TRAVEL THERAPY you need to be strong enough to be alone with your emotions and brave enough to deal with them if they hit you during your downtime, like halfway through your massage.

If you find your answers are split between several categories, lucky you, because you have more TRAVEL THERAPY options to choose from. So let's get started. Pick the trip that fits where you are right now and make the commitment to make a change.

The bottom line is this: It's time to move forward and that's where TRAVEL THERAPY can help. It's not that you can't do it alone; of course you can. But why waste time on the wrong trip when you're likely not thinking too clearly to begin with? With TRAVEL THERAPY, you can change your attitude by changing your environment, and if you choose the right destination you may even change your life!

DESTINATIONS TO AVOID:

- Couples-only or romantic destinations
- Places you went as a couple
- Places you wanted to go as a couple
- Honeymoon destinations
- Wedding destinations

TRAVEL THERAPY SUITCASE SCALE

▲ *The little yellow suitcases are here to let you know, from 1 to 5, how much energy you can expect to exert on your vacation of choice.*

PUSH YOURSELF FORWARD
Daring Destinations

After a breakup you're often left feeling numb, empty inside, helpless, like there's nothing you can do to turn your hopeless life around. Nonsense! This is exactly the kind of self-defeating attitude TRAVEL THERAPY is here to help you avoid. We've all suffered loss, we've all had our hearts ripped out, run over, and shattered into a million pieces, but with TRAVEL THERAPY you can take control of your own destiny and turn things around. It's all about picking a trip to help empower you, a vacation where you can recharge your self-worth and find a way back to your fabulous self.

The trick is hunting down a truly inspiring destination and not just settling for the quick fix of a pretty beach and sweet umbrella drink. After a breakup, lounging around doesn't help. You need the kind of TRAVEL THERAPY that will propel you out of your self-pity and launch you into a new frame of mind. You need a challenge, a BIG challenge!

> *"An adventure undoubtedly has the power to enhance our mood, our biology, and our perspective. Travel has the ability to transform us, from the activation of imagination and self-esteem that happen during the planning stages to the delight during the actual vacation to the lasting imprint on our memories and our very selves."*
>
> —DR. ANTHONY J. TRANGUCH, MD, PhD, PSYCHIATRIST, AND ASSISTANT CLINICAL PROFESSOR OF PSYCHIATRY, COLUMBIA UNIVERSITY

DESTINATION: *Isla Guadalupe*
TRAVEL THERAPY: *Shark Diving*

If the words "Bite me!" come to mind when thinking about your ex, try this terrific—although terrifying—Travel Therapy to help take the bite out of your breakup. Since we're going for it, I mean really going for it, it only makes sense to head to Isla Guadalupe, a volcanic island in the Pacific Ocean off of Baja Mexico, in an area known as one of the top shark diving destinations in the world. Why? It's simple. This is where the big boys play—the great white sharks, the world's largest predatory fish that grows up to five thousand pounds and twenty feet long.

Getting in the water with these fearless creatures is a true test if you're looking to push the envelope—and shove any negative thoughts out of your system. After you accomplish something like sharing the same space with a gigantic creature that can eat you, you'll walk away knowing there's not much you can't handle.

So how do you sign up? It's a lot easier than you might think. Basically, you just need some cash and some serious nerve. Most dives to Isla Guadalupe leave from San Diego, California, and surprisingly, you don't have to be a certified diver to swim with the sharks

▲ *Shark Diving off Isla Guadalupe for Great White Sharks*
SAN DIEGO SHARK DIVING EXPEDITIONS, INC. © JIM CLINKENBEARD

because you're going to be in a cage! Patric Douglas, the CEO of Shark Diver (www.sharkdiver.com), one of the premier operators offering shark dives around Isla Guadalupe, says he wanted to make these dives accessible to everyone. Douglas uses two fifty-square-foot cages and lowers them just below the surface of the water, along with air tubes that pump air to the divers. So all you need is a wetsuit and you're good to go. But Douglas says before you dive off the deep end in this adventure, make sure you're comfortable being in a cage underwater. He says the first time you come face-to-face with a great white it is life-altering. Also check out San Diego Shark Diving Expeditions (www.sdsharkdiving.com), another outfit that does dives in the same general area.

You can find great white dives off South Africa and Australia, but for North America, Isla Guadalupe is the destination of choice because of the great visibility—up to one hundred feet—and the warmer water. Douglas says he's seeing a growing number of women signing up for the adventure, especially successful, single women who are looking for a challenge.

So if you sign up for a dive, how many sharks can you expect to see? Douglas answers this question by talking about his own first dive at Isla Guadalupe, when he wondered the same thing.

"I went down and when I saw six great whites in ten minutes, I was hooked!" Douglas says.

This TRAVEL THERAPY obviously isn't for everyone, but if you're comfortable in the water and looking to challenge your psyche, shark diving is an adventure you shouldn't miss. Douglas summed it up best when he asked, "What do you have to lose except another amazing vacation? You get to walk away feeling like you conquered something, and how great is that?"

"Shark diving changes you. There is nothing quite as exhilarating as getting into the water and looking a great white shark in the eye. The rush that goes through you invigorates and refreshes you, making you feel like you can handle anything that life throws at you."

—CHRISTIE FISHER, IT CONSULTANT, CONCORD, CALIFORNIA

DESTINATION: *San Diego, California*

TRAVEL THERAPY: *Hang Gliding*

If the idea of flying through the air without a plane causes you more stress than excitement, hang gliding probably isn't for you. But if flinging yourself off a cliff and soaring through the sky like a bird is something you've always wanted to try but never found the right moment, now is the perfect opportunity. With this TRAVEL THERAPY, you can literally jump-start your life. One of the greatest things about this experience is it's something you can do alone. Even if you do a tandem flight, it's still just an instructor and you. You don't need a significant other, a friend, or a family member to come along. This is your time, your moment, because when both of your feet leave the ground, it's all about you.

But before you take that first fateful leap, be sure to pick the right school. Research your choice, then research it some more. Make sure you're comfortable with your instructor. I've talked to a lot of experienced hang gliders, and one location they mention over and over again as a tried-and-true favorite is Torrey

Pines in San Diego, California. This is where you'll find one of the oldest hang gliding operations in the country, dating all the way back to 1928. Torrey Pines Gliderport (www.flytorrey.com) is even a San Diego landmark because aviation legend Charles Lindbergh did some of his training there. What I like about the Torrey Pines destination is if you wake up one day and say, "I want to go hang gliding," you don't have to wait weeks to learn all the skills and get certified. You can soar with the seagulls almost immediately by signing up for a tandem flight.

There are other hang gliding schools in the area, too, and San Diego's year-round fabulous weather makes for some fantastic flying conditions. After your thrill ride you can hit the beach or the links at the famed Torrey Pines Golf Club nearby. In this TRAVEL THERAPY, it's all about spreading your wings and reaching new heights and recognizing you really can rise above it all and get over any breakup.

DESTINATION: *Miami, Florida*

TRAVEL THERAPY: *Car Racing*

Everyone start your engines! There's nothing like screaming down a racetrack at breakneck speed to leave your heartache in the

dust. There's a reason racecar drivers walk around looking so cocky and confident. On the track, you'll get in touch with your inner

strength, and you won't even remember how you got off track with your breakup. All around the world, elite racing schools have started offering a true taste of what it feels like to get behind the wheel of pure power. You might hate driving your Honda in traffic, but pushing the pedal to the metal in a high-performance racing machine is an entirely different story.

Miami is a great destination if you're looking for a racing school because this is one city in the south that continues to be a hot spot for high-performance cars and racing. There's a lot of money floating around the Miami area and it has a strong car culture. The weather usually delivers, providing perfect driving conditions, and there are several top schools in the area to choose from. Add it all together and you're good to go!

One of the racetracks you'll want to check out is The Homestead-Miami Speedway, where you not only have the traditional oval course, but you'll also find an infield road course that's used a lot for teaching. Another option is the legendary Sebring International Raceway that's considered one of the most famous tracks in America.

Before you pick your school, you'll want to decide what kind of car you're planning to race around in. Dan Hubbard of the Skip Barber Racing School (www.skipbarber.com) recommends starting with a one- or two-day

driving school using Mazda street cars, but says if you're itching to jump right into racing you can sign up for a class featuring an Indy-style open-wheel Formula racecar or a Mazda MX-5 Cup racecar. Hubbard told me they're seeing more women at the track all the time, and racing classes are set up in a nurturing environment so you can attack the track with finesse and confidence.

Another racing school to scope out is the Homestead-Miami Racing School (www.miamiracingschool.com). Here you can pick how many laps you want to do—from eight to eighty. You can even start off as a passenger, riding with a pro, to get a true taste of how fast these babies can go! Other top schools in the Miami area include the Dale Jarrett Racing Adventure (www.racingadventure.com); the Richard Petty Driving Experience (www.1800bepetty.com); the Jeff Gordon Racing School; and the Mario Andretti Racing School (www.andrettigordon.com).

The bottom line—whatever sparks your engine you can find it in Miami. This is a high-speed TRAVEL THERAPY where you quickly learn that while you can't run away from your problems, you can sure try racing them right out of your system.

▲ *Class in Session at Skip Barber Racing School*
© SKIP BARBER RACING SCHOOL

SWEAT IT OUT OF YOUR SYSTEM
Action Adventures

Endorphins are a beautiful thing. They're neurotransmitters that trigger feelings of euphoria. Pretty cool, huh? What better way to get over a breakup! You can jump-start this natural high in a number of different ways, but one of the easiest is by exercising and working up a sweat to get your heart rate pumping. You've probably heard people talk about a "runner's high," right? Well, the great news is you don't have to run a marathon to kick your endorphins into high gear. Instead, just sign up for the right action adventure trip and let the TRAVEL THERAPY begin!

DESTINATION: *Puerto Rico*
TRAVEL THERAPY: *Zipline Adventure*

Seriously, you have to know you're a little nuts to let someone tie a few ropes around you, hook you onto a skinny cable stretching across the treetops, and launch you off a platform. Nuts, yes, but in a good kind of way. In this TRAVEL THERAPY you're literally pushed out of your safe little world and forced to try something completely new to start the healing process. Talk about channeling your inner Tarzan! Zipping through the trees will definitely get your blood pumping. You'll see your heart still works, even if you thought it was broken after your breakup.

The first time I took the plunge, I was in Puerto Rico on an all-day adventure trip with a group called Acampa Nature Adventures (www.acampapr.com), where zip lining is only one of the many adventures offered. Up to this point in my travels, the only time I ever stopped in Puerto Rico was when I was headed to other Caribbean destinations. When I heard Puerto Rico was turning itself into a new adventure hot spot I thought it was time to check it out. One of the biggest benefits of Puerto Rico is that you don't need a passport if you're coming from the United States—a huge relief for those of you who want to avoid the hassle of going through customs.

Puerto Rico is full of tropical rainforests, and you don't have to travel far outside the main cities to experience an authentic natural

▶ *Zip Lining in the Karst Region of Puerto Rico*
© KAREN SCHALER

environment that's perfect for an adventure trip, especially for zip lining.

When you're standing on the zipline platform you'll probably have a moment when you'll want to turn back. The first time I looked over the edge, I squealed, "Are you kidding me?" My guide laughed good-naturedly. I had the feeling he'd heard this a million times before. Nothing could have prepared me for the first time I stepped off the zipline platform.

It's hard to try and explain the sense of exhilaration you feel as you rocket through the air at about forty miles per hour, screaming across the treetops attached to a tiny cable. The adrenaline rush is intoxicating. You feel like you can conquer the world, like you can do anything. That's why a zipline adventure is the perfect choice for anyone looking for a quick reminder of how life goes on, even after a wretched breakup. Still, you need to be smart about who ties those ropes around you. Safety is a top concern, so always pick a tour that's insured and has certified guides.

> *"Adventure travel should be required for the broken-hearted. The high you get from taking risks and succeeding in your desired experience will always beat out eating chocolate and crying into your pillow!"*
>
> —GRETA PETERS, TRAVEL MEDIA LIAISON, NEW YORK CITY

DESTINATION: *Belize*

TRAVEL THERAPY: *Cave Tubing*

If you're asking yourself, "What the heck is cave tubing?" don't sweat it. You're not alone. Most people have never heard of cave tubing, much less experienced this kind of adventure. This TRAVEL THERAPY truly takes you out of your element and into a part of the world few have ever discovered. Because of this, you'll end up discovering a lot about yourself.

For this trip into the heart of Belize, plan on leaving your diving gear and snorkel mask behind because this water adventure isn't about exploring coral reefs but instead a body of water called Caves Branch River, hidden deep inside a lush Belizean rainforest. There are several tour operators offering cave tubing experiences, but I went with the group at Jaguar Paw Jungle Resort (www.jaguarpaw.com) because it's known as the originator of cave tubing in this part of Belize and because the guides take smaller groups.

Not knowing exactly what to expect on your cave tubing adventure is part of the magic. When you show up you're given a huge inner tube to carry on an easy forty-minute hike through the jungle and down to the river. You'll want to wear shoes that can get wet and to douse yourself with bug spray. Before you get into the water you're given a small headlamp to wear. You'll feel like a coal miner, but trust me, you'll want to wear it; as soon as you're in the river you immediately start floating toward a series of pitch-black caves.

On my cave tubing trip, everyone in the group was talking and giggling and trying to take pictures at first, but as we ventured deeper into the cave we were struck silent and overcome with a sense of peacefulness and awe. When our guide shared stories about the ancient Mayans who used these caves thousands of years before I couldn't help but feel moved by the legacy of my surroundings.

Since it's so dark, the guide starts out in the front, leading the group and instructing everyone to link their feet onto the next closest inner tube until the whole group is floating down the river attached to one another. It's possible to venture off on your own, but always keep an eye on where your group is so you don't get left behind. Floating down the river seems simple enough but then you hit the rapids and start picking up speed. On this part of the trip you're going to have to hold on tight to your inner tub and navigate through some tight corners. It's exhilarating and so different from any experience I've ever had before. You have no choice but to go with the flow and trust where you're going is where you're supposed to be. It's a Travel Therapy lesson about finding yourself by letting go, and trusting that sometimes not knowing what comes next is the best part of the journey.

DESTINATION: *Sun Valley, Idaho*
TRAVEL THERAPY: *Whitewater Rafting*

A sensational way to take your mind off your breakup is to wash that person right out of your system by tackling some rapids in Sun Valley, Idaho. The scenery alone in this Travel Therapy destination will help boost your spirits, and once you're in the raft you won't have time to torture yourself with thoughts of what went wrong during your relationship.

I've traveled to Sun Valley several times in the winter months and always considered this a favorite ski destination, so I was

surprised by all this area has to offer during the summer months when I went there for my first whitewater rafting adventure. There are dozens of different rafting trips you can take down the Salmon and Payette rivers offered by eleven local outfitters. The Salmon River is known as "The River of No Return," so just plan on leaving your old relationship and negative thoughts behind.

Depending on the trip you pick, you can experience everything from cliffs towering more than a thousand feet high to hot springs to Indian pictographs. The best time to go is between June and August, and the further into August you get, the calmer the rapids are.

How do you choose the best trip for you? Easy. The website for the Sun Valley/ Ketchum Chamber and Visitors Bureau (CVB) (www.visitsunvalley.com) always has

▲ *Tackling the Rapids in Sun Valley, Idaho*
© SUN VALLEY/KETCHUM CVB

updated information on specific outfitters and different whitewater rafting options. The folks at the CVB are fantastically friendly and are always standing by, ready to help you out. They recommend picking your trip carefully to match your "nerve" and skill level. The rapids in this area range from class 2 to class 5, with 5 being the toughest. Ask yourself if you are looking to just float down the river calmly or attack the rapids with a vengeance. That's what I love about Sun Valley as a river rafting destination; you have so many different trip options, from tame to treacherous.

If you're looking for the ultimate confidence-booster, don't miss the Middle Fork of the Salmon River. People travel from all over the world to try out this one hundred-mile stretch of pure adrenaline. This is where you can drown your heartache in some wild rapids and emerge a different person! Just remember the key to this TRAVEL THERAPY is to push yourself out of your usual comfort zone. Be safe, but don't play it safe, you know? Don't forget, it's all about challenging yourself and trying something new. Just make sure to stay in the raft!

LICK YOUR WOUNDS AND HEAL
Soothing Spa Escapes

Truth is, sometimes the best thing you can do when you're feeling washed up and worn out is to sneak off to a place where you can hunker down for a while, a place where you can revitalize your mind, body, and soul. If this sounds like one of those fluffy ads for a fancy spa experience, you're right, at least in part. It's not an ad, but going to a luxurious spa for some TRAVEL THERAPY is a smart idea if, and only if, you pick the right destination.

For example, if you've just had your heart handed to you on a platter and you're feeling more alone than you ever have in your life, you probably don't want to head to a romantic spa destination that caters to couples. All that hand holding, kissing, and lovey-dovey stuff is bound to turn your stomach. Your best bet is to pick a spa in a fun or funky location. You can also pick one of the exotic wellness centers where most of the clientele are on their own. Or you can opt for a mini mind adjustment and pick a day spa that's close to you. If you love the idea of pure pampering but hate the idea of spending money on it, you can also save some big bucks by transforming your own home into a spa sanctuary. Whatever your schedule or budget, relax, there's a fluffy robe waiting for you.

DESTINATION: *Phoenix/Scottsdale, Arizona*

The "Valley of the Sun" in the Phoenix/Scottsdale area of Arizona is known as one of the top spa meccas in the world. You could stay here two weeks and go to a different spa every day and still not even make a dent in the long list of top spots. The specialty here is resort spas where pampering is at a premium and the treatments offered are as unique as the desert surroundings.

Seek out the treatments offering natural ingredients from the surrounding environment, like agave and turquoise, because many of these treatments can only be found in Arizona and you wouldn't want to miss your chance to try them out. Since the spa choices can overwhelm, it's best to have a plan and pick one spa as your central base. Then you can either enjoy that spa for your entire stay or venture out and try some different options.

The Phoenix/Scottsdale area is a fantastic pick in the winter if you're in the middle of a deep freeze and you're searching for a way to thaw out. This area rocks in the summer, too, when the temperatures climb but the prices drop dramatically. No matter what time of year it is, there's always something soothing about this desert destination. You're forced to slow down, to relax, and to breathe because so often after a breakup it can feel like you've been holding your breath.

If you're looking for help trying to narrow down the best spa choice for you, two great resources are the Greater Phoenix Convention and Visitors Bureau (www.visitphoenix.com) and the Scottsdale Convention and Visitors Bureau (www.scottsdalecvb.com). Both have fantastic websites jam-packed with information about the different resorts and spas, and they also list upcoming specials you can take advantage of. Once you make a list of your top choices, you can go to the actual spa websites to surf around and see what jumps out at you. You can also find information about the amazing restaurants, shopping, and golf in the area—just another reason why this spa haven is so popular!

Word of advice: Don't stress too much when you're trying to make a choice because at the end of the day it's hard to go wrong in this destination. You'll notice when you're doing your research several spas keep showing up on "best of the best" lists.

Following is a list of some of my favorites. I like to call them the "Sensational Seven." These are spas I've tried personally, and all of them are ideal locations for licking your wounds and healing, so you can walk away with a new frame of mind.

▶ *Revive Spa at JW Marriott Desert Ridge, Phoenix, Arizona*
© JW MARRIOTT DESERT RIDGE RESORT

- Agave Spa—The Westin Kierland Resort & Spa: www.kierlandresort.com
- Alvadora Spa—Royal Palms Resort and Spa: www.royalpalmshotel.com
- Centre for Well-Being—The Phoenician: www.thephoenician.com
- Four Seasons Spa—The Four Seasons at Troon North: www.fourseasons.com /scottsdale

- Revive Spa—JW Marriot Desert Ridge Resort & Spa: www.jwdesertridgeresort.com
- Spa Avania—Hyatt Regency Scottsdale at Gainey Ranch: www.spaavania.com
- Willow Stream Spa—The Fairmont Scottsdale: www.fairmont.com/scottsdale

▲ *Alvadora Spa at the Royal Palms Resort & Spa, Phoenix, Arizona*
© ROYAL PALMS RESORT AND SPA, PHOENIX, ARIZONA

"After a difficult breakup I took a short vacation to Rocky Point in Mexico. I didn't have time to travel far so I packed up my car and headed South with my family. The time spent with my kids, resting and relaxing on the beach, helped me to renew myself after the emotional stress of a breakup. It was rejuvenating and just what I needed."

—Faith Hibbs-Clark, Casting Director for Film and Television,
Los Angeles and Arizona

Talk about a funky, fun spa destination! Lady Vegas is the perfect choice after a breakup because after you're pampered senseless you can venture out knowing there's nothing to lose. You're starting fresh and you're already a winner! Vegas is a town of true transformation. Although it's still known as "Sin City," Las Vegas has elevated its reputation to a world-class, luxurious destination—proving anything is possible!

What I love about Las Vegas as a spa destination is how it's constantly evolving. Just when you think you've seen it all, Vegas jumps up and grabs your imagination with new surprises. This is one destination where you are never bored and you can always count on finding cutting-edge spa treatments.

Las Vegas is a virtual Disneyland of spa choices. You can opt for palatial posh by checking into the luxurious spa at the Bellagio (www.bellagio.com) where the Zen-influenced design creates a contemporary but warm environment. Or, for a more intimate feel, one of my favorite picks is the chic bathhouse spa at THEhotel (www.mandalaybay .com) at Mandalay Bay. Instead of the "bright and light" decor you usually find at spas, the bathhouse is painted in rich dark colors with textured slate walls and chocolate brown wood accents. A massive wall of water is a highlight here, and don't miss soaking in the special submersion pools that you can enjoy before or after your treatment.

If you want to go big, check out the two-story, 69,000-square foot Canyon Ranch SpaClub at the Venetian (www.thevenetian .com), where you'll also find a full fitness center and an indoor rock climbing wall. One of the newest spas on the strip, Qua Baths & Spa at Caesars Palace (www.caesarspalace.com), is also creating quite a stir. I had the chance to walk through this new spa as it was being built, and even then you could feel how sensational it was going to be. Qua Baths & Spa has some truly unique offerings including Roman baths, an Arctic ice room, and a treatment featuring crystal body art.

Vegas never disappoints. There's an infectious energy here that's exhilarating and intoxicating—a winning combination for any TRAVEL THERAPY destination!

DESTINATION: *Los Angeles Area*

The City of Angels can work wonders if you're struggling with a breakup. This is where people come to follow their dreams, and there's a feeling here that at any moment your life can change. As crazy crowded as the L.A. area is, you can create your own peaceful paradise when you check into one of the city's spectacular spas. I mean, come on, think about it. If this area is good enough for Hollywood hotshots, the quality of spa treatments has to be first rate. So why not celebrate like a rock star and sign yourself up for some serious pampering, celebrity style? You deserve it!

The hardest thing you have to navigate is deciding on the perfect spa for you. First, think about the kind of environment you want. Are you looking for something holistic and authentic, or do you want something by the beach, or do you crave some serious bling and want to go glam?

Let's start with the bling. I found a great example of serious glitter and glam at the award-winning spa at the The Peninsula Beverly Hills (www.peninsula.com). This spa is known for its signature precious gem massages during which actual diamonds, rubies, emeralds, and sapphires are used in massage oils to promote everything from healing and tranquility to love and harmony. Sounds tailor-made to help deal with a breakup! During my sapphire massage I was told to "breathe in the love and exhale anger." It felt a little silly at first, but I gave it a shot and in the end, I have to admit, I really did feel better. After your spa treatment, you can relax at the roof garden restaurant where they dish up a delicious spa menu, and if you're looking to indulge, try their fabulous signature mango mojito.

When I'm in L.A., I usually look for spas near the beach because for me the ocean has such a calming effect. Two Santa Monica spas, Le Merigot Hotel and Spa (www.lemerigothotel.com) and ONE, the Spa at Shutters on the Beach (www.shuttersonthebeach.com), are both excellent choices that offer treatments and luscious products inspired by the sea.

If you're looking for a quick fix, a day spa with a laid-back vibe where the surroundings are understated and naturally tranquil, try a quaint little gem called Willow Spa (www.willowspa.com), tucked away in Santa Monica. You might miss the spa at first because from the outside it looks like a charming bungalow. Once you pass through the front door, though, you feel like you're in a tropical village. Willow Spa has a number of Asian-inspired treatments, and if you tell them what you're looking for, what emotion you're trying to deal with (like the pain from a breakup), they can recommend several different options. It's the perfect place to gain some perspective and the strength to deal with whatever comes next.

AUTHOR'S PICK

 DESTINATION: *Bali, Indonesia*

After a breakup, I need the kind of Travel Therapy where I'm pushed to the limit, physically and mentally, and the farther I can fly away from home the better! One summer my best friend and I were both going through some hard relationship issues, so we left our guys at home and traveled halfway around the world to Bali. We were on a tight budget, so part of the challenge was scraping up the airfare and finding a hotel we could afford. We agreed before we left not to spend our time whining about the guys; this vacation was for us! We knew what we wanted in life and we weren't going to accept any less. This wasn't the kind of trip where we planned to lay around on the beach. We needed an adventure, and we wanted to try things we'd never done before. Bali, with its exotic culture and unique customs, didn't let us down. One of the best parts of the trip was hiking through a rainforest down to a river for some whitewater rafting.

Another highlight was our trip through the Ubud Monkey Forest. I still laugh every time I look at the picture of my friend with a giant Balinese long-tailed macaques on her shoulder. A word to the wise: Don't wear white because you'll get dirty fast! You're warned when you walk into the forest not to feed the monkeys and to put any loose objects away because these mischief-makers are notorious thieves. They'll grab anything shiny, and they especially love sunglasses. It's hilarious to watch at first, until you're the one who's robbed. On the tamer side, a trip to Bali wouldn't be complete without visiting some temples and watching woodcarvers work their magic. This exotic Indonesian destination left my friend and I empowered and better equipped to handle what was waiting for us back home.

> *"Traveling to a new or exotic location frees your mind so you can let go of the daily grind and open yourself to a new place and new people. It's about putting yourself out there and allowing yourself to learn and grow from new experiences. When you're going through a hard time the best vacations are ones that empower you and push you to your limits, ones that push you to do something you'd normally never do. If you live in the city go to the country, if you live in the country go to the city, just change your normal routine and that alone could change your life."*
>
> —SARAH EVANS-THELEN, PUBLIC RELATIONS ACCOUNT DIRECTOR, NEW YORK

Heartbreak Hotel Vacation Checklist

CHOOSE TRIPS THAT:

• Inspire

• Empower

• Challenge

• Energize

• Are outside your comfort zone

• Motivate

▶ *Bali at Jimbaran Bay at Four Seasons Resort*
COURTESY: FOUR SEASONS RESORT AT JIMBARAN BAY/KEVIN ORPIN

"Stop worrying about the potholes in the road and celebrate the journey."

—Fitzhugh Mullan

Chapter 2

The Big Chill

You're close to losing it. You're snapping at coworkers, yelling at friends, and frightening your family. Even your pet is starting to stare at you suspiciously. It's time for a break—before you completely crack! When you're stressed to the limit you shut down mentally and physically, so it's absolutely the worst time to try and make an important decision, like where to go on vacation. You usually rush to get away and end up at a second-rate resort, more annoyed than when you started.

This is where TRAVEL THERAPY can help—by giving you three de-stress destination options where chilling out is the name of the game:

- H$_2$O Therapy—Water Retreats
- Privacy Please!—Private Island Escapes
- Just Breathe—Peaceful Playgrounds

Which travel option will help you the most? Just take the TRAVEL THERAPY quiz to find your best fit!

◀ *Diving off Turtle Island, Fiji*
© TURTLE ISLAND, FIJI

TRAVEL THERAPY QUIZ

1. Your ideal vacation is:
   a. Spending time in the water
   b. Quiet and peaceful
   c. Exploring new places

2. You would rather have:
   a. Dinner on a boat
   b. A private picnic on the beach
   c. Discover a new restaurant

3. You would rather buy:
   a. An underwater camera
   b. Designer sunglasses and beach bag
   c. A backpack and walking shoes

4. What sounds best?
   a. An underwater adventure
   b. A beach escape
   c. Exploring unique places

5. You feel more like a:
   a. Fish
   b. Turtle
   c. Curious cat

6. What "suits" you best?
   a. Wet suit
   b. Bathing suit
   c. Hiking or biking suit

7. Your favorite character is:
   a. The Little Mermaid
   b. Robinson Crusoe
   c. Christopher Columbus

8. Your feet are:
   a. Waterlogged
   b. Pedicured
   c. Calloused

9. Your relaxing ride is a:
   a. Boat
   b. Car
   c. Bicycle

10. You can relate best to:
    a. Jacque Cousteau, underwater explorer
    b. The Trumps, Donald and the Gang
    c. Huckleberry Finn, adventurer

TRAVEL THERAPY DIAGNOSIS

If you have mostly "A" answers, *splish splash*, you need some H20 Therapy—pronto—because the water is the one place where you can truly let go and relax. If "B" is your dominant answer, pack your bags and let your friends and family know that you need some Privacy Please!—and sign yourself up for a little private island pampering to help take the sting out of your stress. Finally, if you answered mostly "C," try venturing into the Just Breathe TRAVEL THERAPY options and explore some unique locations where you can find all the stress busters you need.

DESTINATIONS TO AVOID:

- Crowded and noisy destinations
- Places where you have to wait in long lines
- Places with horrible traffic
- Anyplace where you're around what's stressing you out (work, family, etc.)
- Places packed with children
- Destinations with nasty weather (leading to travel delays)
- Overpriced tourist traps

"*Traveling can be likened to a behavioral therapy. Changing the environment around us can help us get unstuck from negative and stressful thoughts. It's hard to say 'I'm so sick of all this traffic' when you're in rural, beautiful Priest Lake, Idaho, eating a huckleberry parfait. It's hard to think to yourself "I'm so lame" or "I'll never do anything interesting" when you are surfing in Lahaina, Maui, or skiing at Mount Bachelor. Travel is a positive way to challenge and change negative thinking patterns.*"

—EDWIN HOLMES, PSYD, CLINICAL PSYCHOLOGY, PORTLAND, OREGON

H₂O THERAPY
Water Retreats

When your life starts to feel like it's too much to handle, there's something almost mythical about diving into another frame of mind by going underwater and discovering a whole new world. Whether you're a certified diver or just someone who loves to put on a snorkel mask and fins, an H₂0 adventure can help wash away your stress and ease your troubled mind. From the moment you leave dry land there's a sense of excitement. You never know exactly what you're going to find or the kind of marine life you'll see. There is one blissful guarantee, though: peace and quiet. In the underwater world there are no traffic jams, no screaming children, no blaring televisions, no telephones. In this world you can hear yourself breathe, and that alone is priceless.

▲ *Diving in Papua New Guinea*
© JEFF WILDERMUTH, WWW.JEFFWILDERMUTH.COM

DESTINATION: *Great Barrier Reef, Australia*

The first time I ever snorkeled was in Australia at the Great Barrier Reef—and I was scared to death. I had just graduated from college and I'd never been very comfortable in the water. I was pretty sure I didn't want to know what was lurking below, but there I was in one of the top diving and snorkeling destinations in the world. A voice in my head kept shouting at me to suck it up. I had traveled halfway around the globe, after all, so how could I even think about missing this experience? (Did I mention I'm also claustrophobic?)

It was one of those moments in my life when I realized that I'd always regret it if I wimped out, so I gave it a shot. The first time I put my face in the water I panicked seeing all these curious fish swimming around me, but then an amazing feeling of awe took over. It was all so beautiful, so different, and completely serene. My fear melted away and so did my stress. I've loved snorkeling ever since.

One reason the Great Barrier Reef, off the coast of Queensland, is such a fantastic TRAVEL THERAPY destination is because it contains the largest collection of coral reefs in the world, with more than four hundred types of coral, close to three thousand coral reefs, fifteen hundred different kinds of fish, and four thousand types of mollusc. Pretty impressive! No wonder it was selected as Australia's first World Heritage Site in 1981.

Another standout quality: The Great Barrier Reef is huge! I mean really huge. It's bigger than the entire country of Italy.

When you start planning your trip, there are dozens of different tour operators offering snorkeling and diving experiences in all price ranges. A great free resource to check out is the Great Barrier Reef Visitors Bureau (www.great-barrier-reef.com), where you can book your trip and also find out about accommodations and smart local dining choices.

If you choose to explore the Great Barrier Reef, plan on taking a boat out to the dive site and spending at least half the day there. You'll want to make sure you have a strong sunscreen that's waterproof. Many snorkelers wear T-shirts because the sun's rays can be blistering. There are some rules you have to follow to help protect the environment and yourself. You're not allowed to hold or touch any part of the reef, and the same goes for touching the marine life. You'll be told to stay at least one meter away from giant clams (something they didn't have to tell me twice) and to avoid the turtles, whales, and sea snakes (ditto). You are allowed to take pictures and video, so if you don't have a camera, borrow one or rent one, because this is one TRAVEL THERAPY you'll want to show off to your friends! Plus, if you get a great shot you can blow it up and frame it and have it nearby for whenever you need to de-stress.

 DESTINATION: *British Virgin Islands, Caribbean*

There are so many wonderful underwater playgrounds in the Caribbean it's hard to keep track, but a TRAVEL THERAPY favorite is in the British Virgin Islands (BVI) where the water is so calm and clear it seems like you can see forever. This area is probably best known for its amazing snorkeling, although there are some great dive sites where you can feed your inner pirate and check out some cool shipwrecks.

One of the most popular snorkeling spots in the BVI is The Baths, just off the island of Virgin Gorda. You access the site by boat but there's also a beach you can swim to where there are some interesting caves and grottos to explore. The first time I snorkeled there I was surprised to find huge granite boulders

▲ *The Baths off Virgin Gorda, British Virgin Islands*
© KAREN SCHALER

jutting out of the water. All the tropical fish love hanging around these rocks, so you'll be in for a real show.

To avoid the crowds in the high season months of December to April, do your snorkeling early in the mornings or late afternoons. Another snorkeling hot spot is an area known as Dog Islands, also near Virgin Gorda.

If you head over to Norman Island you can't go wrong snorkeling at the Indians with its four giant rocks covered in coral that attract hundreds of colorful parrot fish that will swim right up to you. A sensational secluded place to snorkel is Money Bay, just off Norman Island, where you'll find stingrays in some of the clearest water in the Caribbean. If you're looking for angelfish, head over to Little Jost Van Dyke Island and Green Cay where some incredible reef formations attract angelfish by the thousands. This is also a great place to take pictures!

My all-time favorite spot for snorkeling and diving in the BVI is off of Anegada Island at Loblolly Bay. The beaches there are unbelievably beautiful and you'll rarely see more than a dozen people. Even walking into the water you can see the marine life below. This is the perfect place to swim with sea turtles and find giant conch shells, too. Plan to spend the day there and watch your stress disappear.

"I felt trapped and stressed out by so many negative things going on in my life that I had to get away. I ended up going to the Caribbean to see a Jimmy Buffett concert and to fulfill a lifelong dream to swim with dolphins. The relaxing atmosphere and time alone on the beach did wonders for my psyche. I came back refreshed and ready to conquer the world. It's a vacation I will treasure for the rest of my life."

—DENISE NAUGHTON, TELEVISION NEWS PRODUCER, PHOENIX, ARIZONA

 DESTINATION: *Yap, Micronesia*

Yap. Even the name of this TRAVEL THERAPY destination is cool! I've met some professional dive photographers who've traveled all over the world and insist that diving in Yap, Micronesia, is the ultimate underwater experience. The divers I've talked to are always trying to figure out how to go back for another trip. In the diving industry Yap is known as the number one place where you can see manta rays up close, year-round. This alone has elevated Yap to a premier diving destination.

Yap is also famous for its dolphins, tuna, and reef fish. To help plan your diving experience, one great resource is the website of a group called Beyond the Reef (www.diveyap.com). This group has been offering dives in Yap for more than fifteen years. The owner of the dive operation is Dave Vecella, an American transplant who moved to Yap from the Florida Keys in 1990. He proudly told me Yap is unique in so many ways because "the diving in Yap is some of the world's finest, with the resident population of gentle manta rays that come right up to you and seem to want to play."

Vecella fell in love with the destination and never left. "The island is off the beaten track," he says, "so we don't have hordes of dives crowding the dive sites. In fact, if we see another boat on the horizon, we feel crowded."

As relaxing as it is diving and snorkeling there, Yap itself is more than just a water-lover's paradise. It's also an unspoiled gem. There are several small hotels on the island and the people are known to be shy but friendly. Yap is one of four states in the Federated States of Micronesia, just north of the equator. There are more than six hundred islands in the area, but only a few have people living on them. This is a unique part of the world where the concept of stress barely exists. To get a feel for this exotic TRAVEL THERAPY destination, log on to the Visitors Center of the Federated States of Micronesia (www.visit-fsm.org) and surf the site to your heart's content. You'll quickly find the more you learn, the more you'll want to know!

"I work as a middle school counselor so stress is part of the job! During a summer break I ventured off to the tropics to do some snorkeling. The warm sun and the quite breeze quickly replaced the stress and noise in my body and brain. I came back rested, renewed and rejuvenated, and ready to start another school year."

—DEBBIE HOLMES, MIDDLE SCHOOL COUNSELOR, PORTLAND, OREGON

PRIVACY PLEASE!
Private Island Escapes

If leaving your crazy stressed-out life behind and escaping to a private island is something you've always dreamed about, go for it. Make it happen. It's not as impossible as you might think. There are dozens of TRAVEL THERAPY destinations around the world where you can find a resort on a private island that won't break the bank. It still might be a splurge, but it won't require a second mortgage. So just do it—you're worth it.

The fantastic thing about a private island experience is that you're forced to slow down. You don't have to worry about what tour to

▲ *Turtle Island, Fiji*
© TURTLE ISLAND, FIJI

take, which restaurant to pick, or what to wear. On a private island your choices are blissfully limited, so you can just relax. This is the ideal Travel Therapy choice if you're in a place in your life where you're suffering from sensory overload, bombarded by decision making every day, or looking for a quick vacation fix. It starts with turning off your BlackBerry and leaving your computer behind. Don't worry; it will all be waiting for you when you get home. After your initial withdrawal wears off you might even find you don't miss it at all.

 DESTINATION: *Turtle Island, Fiji*

You have to love the idea of staying at a place where the toughest decision you'll have to make is what kind of tropical drink to order. Now that's a stress-free Travel Therapy vacation! In the Fiji islands you'll find some amazing private islands to choose from—with Turtle Island topping the list. When you visit Turtle Island, it's hard to believe that it was once overrun by wild goats. Now it's a world-class luxury destination and the perfect place to unwind and kick back.

You go to a private island resort because you're looking for peace and quiet, and Turtle Island doesn't disappoint. With only fourteen "bures" (two-room thatched cottages) and fourteen beaches, you'll rarely see another guest. At times you'll feel like you almost have the whole island to yourself. Still, if *almost* isn't good enough, and you're searching for that truly "private" experience, you can rent out the entire island. That's right, just for you. Now we're talking!

A lot of people do this for weddings or business retreats, which is why if you're planning to visit, you need to book early to make sure space is available.

Turtle Island is quiet, but that doesn't mean it's boring. When you're staying on this island there's a long list of activities you can sign up for, including: Horseback riding, hiking, mountain biking, sailing, kayaking, snorkeling, windsurfing, deep-sea fishing, scuba diving, and don't miss the sunset cruise. A favorite activity of mine, though, is simply relaxing on the beach with a good book and one of those yummy umbrella drinks.

The island is tiny, just five hundred acres, but you can still get a relaxing massage and experience gourmet meals and fine wines, proving once again that size isn't everything!

 DESTINATION: *Scrub Island, British Virgin Islands*

It's always exciting to discover a new private island paradise, and Scrub Island has all the makings of a true TRAVEL THERAPY superstar! The resort is scheduled to open in 2009 and will be the first new property in the BVI in more than a decade. Unlike some smaller TRAVEL THERAPY destinations, this new development is substantially larger with a focus on amenities. There will be a hotel along with some standalone ocean view villas. There are also plans to build some cool spa bungalows for those who want to continue their pampering 24/7.

Scrub Island is easy to get to—it's just a short, five-minute ferry ride from the island of Tortola, which most major airline carriers

serve. Usually, the only way you can get to the best private islands in the Caribbean is by boat or private helicopter, so this ferry option is a plus.

Originally, when the developers were starting their plans for Scrub Island, they were thinking about naming the resort The Mainsail. Later they decided to go with the island's original name, Scrub Island. It's not as sexy, but it's more authentic.

Where some of the other private islands in the Caribbean are geared toward total seclusion and privacy, Scrub Island prides itself

▲ *Scrub Island Resort, British Virgin Islands*
© SCRUB ISLAND RESORT

in offering some unique amenities. A spa is planned for this 230-acre island along with a fitness center, three swimming pools, a wine and cigar bar, and even an amphitheater. When the development is done, no more than two hundred people will be allowed to live on the island at one time with the goal of trying to preserve a genuine getaway experience. This is one TRAVEL THERAPY destination worth keeping an eye on.

DESTINATION: *Desroches Island, Seychelles*

You know you're onto something when you find a great island hideaway that royalty and celebrities are known to escape to. This is just one reason why Desroches Island makes the TRAVEL THERAPY list as a perfect de-stress destination. So exactly where is this island? Desroches is part of the Amirante Islands in the Outer Islands of the Seychelles. As the largest of the Amirante Islands, Desroches is about four miles long and is covered with lush vegetation and coconut palms. This remote island is one of those rare slices of paradise where unspoiled beaches seem to stretch on forever and the water is such an amazing turquoise blue it almost seems surreal. There are more than a dozen classified reef sites nearby, making this a favorite stop for divers and deep-sea fishermen.

On the island you'll find the private and exclusive Desroches Island Resort (www .slh.com), a favorite with the jet set. But this resort isn't just about glitz and glam. Instead, this simple but sophisticated property has a laid-back vibe. This resort is set up to provide a peaceful respite where you can forget about the outside world and concentrate on finding yourself. The fact that it's all-inclusive (meals, drinks, water sports) makes it that much easier.

With only twenty suites on the island, there's an intimate feeling and it's not unusual for people to spend the entire day relaxing at the beach, soaking up the soothing atmosphere. If you're craving a massage or facial, you can sign up for a spa treatment, and if you're looking for some activity, you can grab one of the complimentary bikes and explore the island. Feeling more adventurous? Try kayaking, windsurfing, or pedal boats. For a fun change of pace there's also boccie ball, beach volleyball, and tennis. You're not going to get bored on this island, unless you want to be!

▶ *Desroches Island, Seychelles*
© DESROCHES ISLAND, SEYCHELLES, SMALL LUXURY HOTELS OF THE WORLD

STUFF IT! *PACKING TIPS*

There's nothing more stressful than planning the perfect vacation and having your luggage not show up! You immediately go into hyperpanic mode because you packed a prescription (a big no-no) or something you absolutely needed for the trip and now you're out of luck. If you've ever had this happen, you know that you'll end up spending your vacation stressed out because you're trying to track down your luggage. That's why one of the cardinal Travel Therapy rules is: DON'T CHECK YOUR BAGS! I can already hear the squeals of protest. You're thinking that there's absolutely no way you can get everything into a carry-on bag, right? Well think about it—how much better off will you be if none of your luggage shows up? At least when you bring a carry-on, although you can't pack as much, you're guaranteed that what you do pack will actually make it there.

It's alarming the number of bags airlines lose every year, and many bags are never found. Maybe you've been lucky so far, but the numbers don't lie, and it's just a matter of time before you're a lost luggage victim. I've traveled on three-week and longer vacations and managed to just pack a carry-on. The key is to keep your wardrobe simple, roll everything up to make more space, and only pack two or three pairs of shoes.

If you're thinking there's no way to pack all your toiletries because of the new liquid container rules that restrict how much you can carry on, think again. Go through your normal overnight bag and toss half the stuff out. Do you really need seven lipsticks for a weekend getaway? Pare it down. Bring one purse, not five, and leave behind anything you can easily buy where you're going. It's more fun having new stuff anyway. Of course, there are those rare times when you have to check a bag because you're bringing along your golf clubs (seriously, consider renting, it's a great way to demo clubs) or because you need your bike or surfboard (again, consider renting!). If you must, go ahead and check them in but have a backup plan in case they never show up. Don't let lost luggage ruin your trip.

JUST BREATHE
Peaceful Playgrounds

Sometimes when you're stressed out you forget to breathe. Seriously, have you ever been in that situation when your heart feels like it's going to jump out of our chest and your stress is boiling over? Check yourself—you're probably holding your breath. Sometimes you get so used to dealing with your stress you don't even realize what it's costing you until it's too late. That's why choosing the right TRAVEL THERAPY destination is critical.

If you're looking for a peaceful escape that's not entirely isolated, where you still have new places to discover and explore, check out the following TRAVEL THERAPY destinations and learn how to really breathe again!

> *"A place I head if I need to exhale and shake off some stress is the Florida Keys. The beaches, the ocean, and the friendly people make it easy to relax. The best part is taking home the memory of a Florida sunrise and keeping it close whenever I need to regroup."*
>
> —MARYBETH JACOBY, NEWS MANAGER, JACKSONVILLE, FLORIDA

 DESTINATION: *Florida Keys, Florida*

One of the things I've always liked about the Florida Keys is that you can feel like you're in the Caribbean without ever leaving the United States. This destination is a fantastic TRAVEL THERAPY choice if the idea of traveling out of the country causes you even more stress. We're trying to help you get rid of your stress, not create more! So if you're looking for a tropical island escape that doesn't require a passport, grab your bathing suit and flip-flops and head south.

With more than 1,500 islands, the Keys is one of those destinations where the number of relaxing places to visit are limitless. If you're not sure where to start, a great resource is the official tourism council's website for the

Florida Keys (www.fla-keys.com). Here you can find valuable information on the different destinations and lodging options. It will also give you a feel for the different islands so you can pick the spot that calls out to you.

One of my favorite stress busters is Duck Key, right in the heart of the Florida Keys, just ninety miles south of Miami. This sixty-acre island retreat is small enough to have an intimate feel but still offers a lot to see and do. You have the benefit of being surrounded by the Atlantic Ocean and the Gulf of Mexico, so temperatures throughout the year are usually between 75 and 85 degrees.

One place to stay is Hawks Cay (www.hawkscay.com). I knew the first time I checked in that this was just the kind of place for unwinding and kicking back. The hotel has 177 rooms, plus more than a dozen suites. If you're traveling with friends or family your best bet is to rent one of the two- or three-bedroom villas. There are more than two hundred villas on the property, but my favorites are the "preferred villas" that sleep up to eight people. You'll end up feeling like you have a home in the Keys. Some of the villas, like the two-bedroom sanctuary villas, even have their own swimming pools.

So what else is there to do here? Plenty! If you want to try your luck at deep-sea fishing there are several great charters to choose

▲ *Swimming with Dolphins at Hawks Cay, Florida*
© KAREN SCHALER

from that take off right from Hawks Cay's full-service marina. You can also go reef fishing or try a full day of mahi mahi fishing. Another great way to beat your stress is to do some kayaking or parasailing. This is also your chance to swim with Atlantic bottlenose dolphins, and believe me, you'll forget about your problems when you're around these amazing creatures.

Another one of my favorite ways to relax is sailing, and you can learn all the ropes at Steve and Doris Colgate's Offshore Sailing School (www.offshore-sailing.com). You can sign up right at the resort. Depending on the amount of time you have and how much you want to learn, this unique sailing program has you covered.

The perfect way to end your day is by toasting your fabulous self at the Rum Bar where the Caribbean vibe continues with signature drinks featuring unique kinds of rum. Don't miss the mojitos—they're about as authentic as you're going to find without going to Cuba!

 DESTINATION: *Nantucket Island, Massachusets*

Martha's Vineyard always seems to get all the attention when it comes to East Coast island escapes, and don't get me wrong—it's a fantastic destination. But if you're looking to take it down a notch and want a slower pace, Nantucket is where you want to go.

The first time I visited Nantucket I was there for a charity fishing and golf tournament. Our days were so packed full of activities that I barely had a chance to sneak away and enjoy the island. But what I saw of this old whaling port was enough to know I wanted to come back.

Quaint is one of the words that always come to mind when I think of Nantucket. Just thirty miles south of Cape Cod, this island is known as a summer reprieve. I like visiting the island in the colder winter months when all the tourists have gone home. When the temperatures drop, most of the hotels and bed-and-breakfasts cut their rates in half. All you need to do is bundle up a little and you can enjoy the island's 17th-century charm at a fraction of the price. Another bonus about visiting the island in the fall and winter months is that you can find some great holiday gift ideas. Nantucket is known for its phenomenal shopping with streets lined with interesting art galleries, boutiques, and clothing and jewelry stores.

About three miles wide and fourteen miles long, Nantucket only has one town—and you guessed it, it's called Nantucket. Almost 40 percent of the island is protected conservation land and in many places you can still see the architectural influence of the 17th century. Nantucket is small and safe, making it the kind of TRAVEL THERAPY destination where you can pack a weekend bag and come alone or plan a romantic escape or even bring the family. There's something here for everyone.

To help you plan, the Nantucket Island Chamber of Commerce has an excellent website (www.nantucketchamber.org) offering up some interesting information about the island, including everything from the island's unique history to the top places to stay, eat, and shop. Also, don't miss the Nantucket Visitors Services (www.nantucket -ma.gov), where you can always find updated information and a local phone number to call for advice. Both websites can help you figure out if you want to take a ferry to the island, like most people do, or come over in a commuter plane.

Regardless of how you get to Nantucket, you'll notice the soothing influence of the island as soon as you arrive. As simple and understated as Nantucket is, there's also big money here. Every year more wealthy visitors are coming to Nantucket, falling in love with the island, and snatching up property and homes in the area. Some locals worry about how these cash-flush visitors will impact Nantucket's old world appeal, but so far Nantucket has stayed true to its historical roots, and hopefully it will continue to stay that way.

 DESTINATION: *Tulum, Mexico*

There are some incredible places to visit in Mexico, but if you're not careful you can end up in an overpriced tourist trap, sucking down a horrible margarita made with cheap tequila. When you're stressed to the limit it's easy to just rush to get out of town and pick a place you've heard of, or pick one of those all-inclusive specials that's advertised in the newspaper. It's quick, it's simple, but it could also be disastrous. You could wind up at a hideous place that taints your judgment of Mexico. It's not fair to you, and it's certainly not fair to Mexico! You can find some of the most beautiful and interesting TRAVEL THERAPY destinations just south of the border if you know where to go and get off the beaten track.

On my first trip to Tulum in 2005, I was a little skeptical. I had only heard a few things about this tiny seaside Mexican town. I knew there was a "rustic" holistic spa, so that's where I was headed. I had heard the beach, a popular spot for backpackers and campers, was amazing. I also knew Tulum was famous for its Mayan ruins and that some interesting hotels and restaurants were starting to pop up in the area.

I flew into Cancun, and since this was supposed to be a relaxing spa vacation, I bypassed the hassle of renting a car and arranged to have a driver pick me up at the airport for the hour and a half trip south to Tulum. Hiring a private driver isn't much more than a taxi, so it's worth checking out. We didn't drive very far before I had no cell phone signal. About two hours later we turned off the main road onto a bumpy dirt road. I was deep in the jungle and there wasn't another car in sight. I couldn't help but worry that if I disappeared no one would ever find me. Ironically, what I was worried about when I first arrived turned out to be what I ended up loving most about this destination. You're isolated, but you're far from lost.

While the small town of Tulum is bustling with tiny inexpensive restaurants and souvenir shops, most of the resorts are hidden away down unmarked dirt roads, secluded and definitely off the beaten path. For years backpackers and campers have enjoyed Tulum's stunning beaches, but now the area is almost unrecognizable with new resorts cropping up each year. If you're still looking for an authentic choice, Cabanas Copal (www.cabanascopal.com) is one of the original Tulum resorts where you have close to fifty simple cabanas hidden in the jungle, many with Caribbean views. There is no electricity here, so for light you're given candles. You'll

also need to bring a flashlight to get around at night. Two other intimate Tulum properties are Zahra (www.zahra.com.mx) and Azulik (www.azulik.com). Zahra has about two-dozen cabanas, which have electricity between sunrise and 11 PM. Some of the newer cabanas have floor to ceiling windows with amazing views of the Caribbean. Azulik is the place to go if you want privacy. It's probably the most visually stunning location because there are fifteen seaside cabanas that are built so close to the water you can throw a rock and hit the waves. You're back to using candles at this property, but you won't even mind because this little beauty is known as a romantic couple's escape. The vibe here is rustic chic. The rooms all feature swinging lounge beds, along with your normal bed. There are floor to ceiling windows overlooking the Caribbean, and out on your private deck you have a tiny tiled hot tub and a hammock. I spent a lot of time in the hammock! If you want to order anything from room service you just leave a flag on your front door and someone will come by eventually. Nothing happens very fast here.

For meals, all three of these properties share several covered outdoor restaurants, so you always have a variety to choose from. At night you'll want your flashlight handy because only candles light your way and it gets pitch-dark in the jungle. You'll also want to keep track of where you're going because it's easy to get lost. The properties are so small so you will always find your way back to your cabana eventually. When I was there almost everyone I met were honeymooners or couples who told me they had searched the world over to find this kind of rustic intimate escape. I didn't see anyone who was stressed out trying to find an Internet connection or cell service or complaining because they didn't have a television in their room.

If the surroundings alone aren't enough to ease all your tension, you can just make your way through the jungle to the Maya Spa where the menu options are as unique as the surroundings. Most of your treatments are done outside, either at the beach, in the jungle, or on top of a small cliff overlooking the water. There's a heavy emphasis on Mayan healing techniques that help relax your mind and body. It may take a few days to get used to the simplicity of your surroundings, but once you finally let go it's liberating. In Tulum, you realize that sometimes the simplest things in life are the most satisfying and that less is often more.

AUTHOR'S PICK

 DESTINATION: *Sardinia, Italy*

I'll never forget my trip to Sardinia because it was insane. It was the middle of summer— the absolute worst time to travel to Europe because of the crowds and high prices—when a friend called completely frazzled and begged me to go on a trip with her. In all the years I'd known her she wasn't the type to stress out or to ask for help, so I knew this was big and I couldn't say no. Besides, I had just quit my job and wasn't sure where I was going next, so I was free to travel. Free but broke.

My friend had her heart set on Italy, a favorite country of both of ours, and since we both knew we'd be shelling out a sick amount of money, we decided to go all out and travel to Sardinia, an island just off of Italy's coast, the second largest island in the Mediterranean after Sicily.

Since we were already splurging, we decided to stay in a posh area in northern Sardinia called Costa Smerelda (the Emerald Coast), the land of luxe and big bucks. Somehow we found a hotel we could afford (at least on our credit cards) in fashionable Porto Cervo, so we were off. We both agreed not to whine about how much this trip was costing and to just enjoy the experience. It might sound irresponsible, but how can you put a price tag on your peace of mind? We jokingly rationalized that therapy would have cost more than the trip so we were actually saving money!

It was worth every cent! Sardinia is truly magical. (For a preview try www.sardinia. net and www.discover-sardinia.com.) There was so much to see that we decided to rent a car and couldn't stop laughing when the guy delivered this itty-bitty thing that looked more like a go-cart. Was he kidding? No. It was one of those Smart cars that are only about three feet tall and six feet long. It was ridiculous looking. We had wanted "economy," and that's exactly what we got. Every time we drove up a hill, and there are a lot of them in Sardinia, we felt like we needed to start peddling. Still, it got us where we wanted to go.

After exploring the island by car, we decided it would be a sin not to get out and see Sardinia from the water. So we scraped our pennies together and rented a boat and a driver for a half-day so we could do some snorkeling and exploring. Surrounded by gorgeous beaches, Sardinia is known as one of the top yachting destinations in the world so our mini-boat ride was by far the best investment of our trip. Our driver didn't speak a lick of English, but he gave us a good deal and seemed happy to point out the sights, even though we had no idea what he was talking about. He won our hearts when he brought out some Chianti for lunch and we all toasted a trip of a lifetime. On the flight home we both felt empowered. Our spontaneous trip was just what we needed to help let go of all the stress from the past and forge ahead to a better future.

The Big Chill Vacation Checklist

CHOOSE TRIPS WHERE YOU CAN:

- Relax
- De-stress
- Recharge
- Go with the flow
- Reenergize
- Regroup

"There ain't no surer way to find out whether you like people or hate them than to travel with them."

—Mark Twain

Chapter 3

Ready For Romance

*A*re you ready for romance? I mean really ready? Whether you're trying to figure out if the person you're with is the one you want to spend the rest of your life with, or whether you're searching for new ways to spice up your love life and add some sizzle to your relationship, a couple's vacation can do the trick—if you choose the right destination.

So many couples pick a place where the guys go off and do their own thing, like golfing or fishing, and the women spend the day at the spa or shopping. With a vacation like this the only real quality time you have together is when you meet up for meals. Even worse, you decide to vacation with another couple so it turns into one big party instead of the special "one-on-one" time you need to see if you're truly compatible. It might be a fun trip, but it's not the kind of trip where you two can bond with each other.

To help avoid these common pitfalls, TRAVEL THERAPY has some enticing options where your relationship and romance is front and center:

- Serve Up the Sizzle—Romantic Destinations
- A Pirate's Life—Sailing Adventures
- Houdini Vacations—Quick Weekend Escapes

How do you pick? Take the TRAVEL THERAPY quiz and pack your bags!

◀ *Las Ventanas al Paraiso, a Rosewood Resort, Los Cabos, Mexico*
© LAS VENTANAS AL PARAISO, LOS CABOS, MEXICO

TRAVEL THERAPY QUIZ

1. For a couple's vacation you want:
   a. Time alone
   b. Some adventure
   c. A quick escape

2. As a couple you like to:
   a. Lounge on the beach
   b. Spend time on a boat
   c. Get away for just a day

3. You like:
   a. Beach vacations
   b. Exotic and adventuresome trips
   c. Quick weekend getaways

4. The song that says it best is:
   a. "Margaritaville"
   b. "Come Sail Away"
   c. "Day Tripper"

5. The phrase that best describes you is:
   a. Have passport, will travel
   b. Have passport, where's the boat?
   c. Have passport, will travel, but make it fast

6. Your ideal vacation is to:
   a. A couple's beach hideaway
   b. Sailing and boating destinations
   c. A luxury resort that doesn't take ten hours to get to

7. On trips together you are:
   a. Looking for a sure bet
   b. Willing to try something new
   c. Wanting to stay close to home

8. For your couple's vacations you like:
   a. Everything planned
   b. To go with the flow
   c. Travel to be quick and easy

9. Right now you have time to get away:
   a. for at least a week
   b. for more than a week
   c. only for the weekend

TRAVEL THERAPY DIAGNOSIS

If you've selected mostly "A" answers, get ready to wiggle your toes in the sand because an exotic beach vacation is just what you need to relax as a couple and get away from it all. You'll want to check out destinations under Serve Up the Sizzle because these sexy and sultry romantic escapes are so secluded you'll have plenty of intimate time together. If "B" is your favorite pick, get your sea legs ready and try a trip under A Pirate's Life. On these sensational sailing adventures your close quarters on the boat mean you'll have no other choice than to really get to know your partner. If you don't have a lot of time to spend then you probably answered "C" for many questions. No worries, you still can fit in romance with some fantastic Houdini Vacations.

DESTINATIONS TO AVOID:

- Family-friendly destinations
- Crowded all-inclusive resorts
- Golf resorts (unless you both golf)
- Loud and noisy destinations
- Unromantic destinations
- Party central resorts
- Resorts where your friends are going

"Traveling the world, or just really wonderful parts of it, encourages both flexibility and adaptability. People in other places do things so differently! What a wonderful therapeutic reminder that there are many different ways of going through life that can provide comfort and inspiration."

—MICHAEL D. YAPKO, PhD, CLINICAL PSYCHOLOGIST
AND AUTHOR, FALLBROOK, CALIFORNIA

SERVE UP THE SIZZLE
Romantic Destinations

When was the last time you kicked back and spent hours with the person you love, just the two of you with no kids, friends, computers, cell phones, or television? If you're still sitting there trying to figure it out, chances are you're more than ready for a vacation where the focus is all about spending time with each other, with no distractions. If this sounds fabulous but unrealistic, have some faith. There are some amazing TRAVEL THERAPY destinations where having private time together as a couple is not only possible but practically mandatory.

Ask yourself this: How much longer can you afford to go on feeling disconnected and distant? Isn't it worth making the extra effort to travel to a romantic destination that can help inspire you again, bringing you both closer together until the two of you remember and appreciate why you picked each other in the first place? Let TRAVEL THERAPY help you find your way.

DESTINATION: *Riviera Maya, Mexico*

Hola, romance! The real beauty of Mexico's Riviera Maya is that this destination hot spot is new on the romance circuit. Besides the big beautiful hotels that attract families and singles, you can also find some charming hidden boutique properties that specialize in catering just to couples. These beautiful resorts only have a few rooms scattered around the lush property so you feel like the "real" world is thousands of miles away. This is the perfect place to get away and reconnect with the one you love. Another bonus—there are great deals to be found in this part of Mexico, so you can splurge and not feel guilty.

So where exactly is this little slice of heaven? The Riviera Maya runs along the Caribbean, stretching about one hundred miles south from Cancun to Tulum. The easiest way to get there is to fly into Cancun and either rent a car or have your resort arrange for someone to pick you up. Since this trip is all about relaxing and spending time with each other, I'd recommend the pickup route so you don't have to hassle with renting a car. This way you don't have to worry about

arguing over directions, and if you want a car later your resort can always set that up.

When you're first going along coastal Highway 307, it's hard to see the beauty of this area because the Caribbean is hidden behind a thick emerald green jungle. On my first trip to the Riviera Maya I was pretty skeptical. From the highway it looked awfully bleak and didn't seem very relaxing to me as we zigzagged in and out of traffic!

I quickly learned the magic comes when you turn down one of the dirt roads and venture toward where the water is. The first time you see the turquoise waves it's breathtaking. There's this awesome sense of discovery when you know you've found something special— your very own sliver of paradise.

▲ *The Tides Riviera Maya Resort, Playa del Carmen, Mexico*
© THE TIDES RIVIERA MAYA RESORT, KOR HOTEL GROUP

Choosing the right place to stay is critical when you're planning a romantic rendezvous. It's true that on many trips you don't really care about your room because you're never there, but on this TRAVEL THERAPY vacation your room is important because it will set the tone for your entire trip. That's why the property you pick is so crucial. You don't want to end up trying to relax by the pool with a bunch of screaming children running around, and this is not the time to be surrounded by a bunch of college students downing tequila shots.

For a couple's vacation your best bet is selecting one of the smaller resorts where you rarely see children and where the luxurious surroundings will make you feel pampered from the moment you arrive. One of my favorite properties is Maroma (www.maromahotel.com) in Puerto Morelos. The Hollywood A-list crowd has known about this beachfront beauty for years, but now the secret is out and more couples are learning about this hot little property.

Maroma's sixty-five rooms range from guest rooms in the main hacienda to lavish private suites. If privacy is what you're looking for, the suites are the way to go. Many of the suites even have their own private rooftop massage area and workout gym. One of my favorite ways to spend the day is lounging on the giant beach beds, right next to the water. You can unwind with your significant other while you sip signature cocktails and nibble on ceviche. This is also the perfect place to watch the sunset and celebrate your relationship under the stars.

An equally fabulous TRAVEL THERAPY choice is the Tides Resort (www.tidesriviera maya.com) in Playa del Carmen. This beachfront honeymooner's favorite has thirty villas tucked away in the jungle. At nighttime, the entire property is bathed in candlelight. Tiny candles and lanterns are set up throughout the property so you feel like you're walking into a scene from a romance novel. It only gets better when you get to your villa. Each one is decorated with traditional Mayan touches, giving it an almost mythical ambience. One of the highlights is your own private plunge pool where you can cool off together before snuggling on your outdoor daybed or hammock.

The spa on the property is also worth checking out because you'll find several unique couple's treatments and you can sign up for a private Mayan dinner where the resort's chef shares age-old cooking secrets. On your first night you might get lost trying to find your jungle villa because they're all hidden so discreetly throughout the resort, but that's part of the charm. You will quickly learn that sometimes getting lost is the best way to really find each other again.

For more options on romantic escapes along the Riviera Maya, the Mexican Tourism Board has set up a great website at www.visit mexico.com. Here you'll find links to different hotels and insider information about the best places to stay and current travel deals.

DESTINATION: *Peter Island, British Virgin Islands*

With warm weather, beautiful beaches, and scenery to die for, the Caribbean has dozens of special destinations where you can hide away with a loved one, but a TRAVEL THERAPY standout has always been Peter Island. From the first time I visited this exclusive private island in the early 1990s, I knew, without a doubt, there was something special here. When you're staying on the island you're so secluded you feel like you have the entire island to yourself. The beaches look like something out of a fairytale and the sand is so soft it feels like talcum powder. This is the kind of destination that's so spectacular your troubles seem to melt away and you can concentrate on each other.

Surrounded by yachts, catamarans, and sailboats, this island has always been known as a sailor's paradise. Unlike many destinations that get "discovered" and then slowly lose their charm, Peter Island is like a fine wine: It only gets better with time. This private island excels at providing the perfect backdrop for romance and relaxation,

and you can't help but reconnect when surrounded by such beauty.

To get to the island you can fly into the airport at Tortola in the British Virgin Islands, where someone from the resort can meet you and take you on a private launch to the island. There's also a ferry you can take on select days if you're coming from St. Thomas. If you're sailing or yachting, Peter Island has a deep-water marina with fifteen slips. You can also arrive by helicopter from San Juan or St. Thomas and land on the island's private heliport.

There's only one small resort on the island with fifty-two rooms and four luxury villas. The new six bedroom, Falcon's Nest Villa that sits perched 350 feet above the Caribbean was unveiled in 2008 as the ultimate splurge. The idea of Peter Island is to keep it small and intimate. In addition to its five private beaches, you'll also find a world-class spa, tennis courts, and a long list of water sports to keep you busy if you want to do more than kick back on the beach.

Set on eighteen hundred luscious acres, this is the place to come if you want to spend time together as a couple but not be around hundreds of other people. Peter Island is tranquility incarnate, and one of the best things is that you can do absolutely nothing and feel like you're having the vacation of a lifetime! The staff is legendary for going above and beyond to make sure you have everything you need and can even set you up with a romantic picnic on the beach or candlelight dinner.

If you really want to go all out, try renting one of the villas. The smallest at 3,626 square feet is called Hawk's Nest and is up

▲ *Peter Island Resort, British Virgin Islands*
© KAREN SCHALER

on the hillside with panoramic water views. Regardless of where you stay, an ideal way to end your day is a moonlight stroll on the beach. You'll quickly find the only downfall to this TRAVEL THERAPY destination is that you won't want to go home!

DESTINATION: *Pangkor Laut, Malaysia*

There's always something so exciting and intoxicating about traveling to an exotic location like Malaysia, where the customs and culture are amazingly different. If you experience these differences as a couple, it can help bring you closer together by forming a common bond and understanding. If you can open your mind and heart to new travel experiences, the possibilities are endless. No matter where you are in the world, you can find romance if you look in the right place.

Of course, it doesn't hurt to pick a private island that's world-famous for its spa, beach, and two million-year-old rainforest. At Pangkor Laut Resort in Malaysia you'll find a rare mix of a tropical beach vacation and a true jungle experience. On this property there are 142 luxury villas and suites with the highlight being the signature sea villas that are perched impressively on stilts above the crystal clear water. If you want to be on dry land, you can choose a beach villa where you're just seconds away from the surf or head to the hillside where there are villas tucked away in the rainforest.

The island of Pangkor Laut is just off the west coast of Malaysia and you can find all the information about how to get there on the resort's website (www.pangkorlautresort.com).

Because this destination is so far away, a lot of savvy travelers spend a few days exploring Malaysia and then head over to Pangkor Laut for a peaceful place to wind down. Besides the usual beach activities, you can also set up a trip through the rainforest and do some kayaking.

A stay at the resort wouldn't be complete without trying out the world-famous spa. The Spa Village has a long list of signature treatments for both men and women that are inspired by the surrounding environment and Asian culture. What makes this spa so perfect for couples is that there are close to a dozen treatment pavilions where you can enjoy your treatments together and then share an oversize sunken tub, outdoor showers, and a private deck. Couples travel from all over the globe just to experience this spa, so even if you're not exactly the "spa couple," you might want to make an exception and try this one out!

If you're going for a sunny, warm Travel Therapy destination where you're going to be around a lot of water, you need to be sure to take the right sunscreen with you. There's nothing less romantic than a horrible sunburn that hurts so much you don't want anyone to touch you. Here's how to protect yourself:

- Apply at least 15 SPF thirty minutes before going into the sun.

- Reapply after swimming even if it's waterproof.

- Use a handful to cover your entire body—don't scrimp.

- Pick a broad-spectrum brand that protects against UVA and UVB rays.

- Wear a hat, sunglasses, and extra protection on your face.

- Don't forget your nose, ears, hands, feet, and hard-to-reach places.

- Make sure the sunscreen is not expired because ingredients can degrade.

A PIRATE'S LIFE
Sailing Adventures

Of all the TRAVEL THERAPY vacations, sailing is one of my favorites. It really doesn't make any sense when you consider I'm claustrophobic and not entirely comfortable in the water, but there's something so magical and romantic about gliding across the waves with the wind in your hair that always keeps me craving more. I've learned, sometimes the hard way, that who you decide to take on your trip can make or break your sailing vacation. Be forewarned. This kind of TRAVEL THERAPY is a true test of any relationship. If you really want to get to know someone, try being confined on a small boat together for a week. I always say sailing is a great litmus test and something you should do before you get married. If you can't sail together, how do you plan to spend a life together? Whether you decide to hire a captain or sail yourself, you'll be spending a lot of time with just each other. That's the whole idea. Remember, this is supposed to be a romantic trip!

In the evenings when you're anchored down for the night, sometimes the only entertainment you'll have is each other. This is a time when you can simply talk and share ideas and dreams; read; play cards or backgammon; or just relax under the stars. Think of your boat as a floating hotel where every day your scenery changes. Living A Pirate's Life is simple if you're both on the same page, and if you find out you're not, there's always the dinghy one of you can take to shore!

"My boyfriend (now husband) and I chartered a boat along the Turkish coast for a week. It was so serene and peaceful. The water was crystal clear. Much of the coastline was underdeveloped and uninhabited but occasionally we'd dock at a small seaside town to shop and have dinner. Our boat's staff—a captain, cook, and deckhand—were accommodating and respectful of our space and the food was always fresh and delicious. It was truly a relaxing and memorable experience that we hope to repeat someday."

—KIRSTEN GETZELMAN, VP FINANCE DIRECTOR,
BRENTWOOD, CALIFORNIA

 DESTINATION: *Turkey*

Deciding where to go on your sailing vacation can be just as important as who you take. If you're looking for a unique experience, Turkey offers up some of the best sailing in the world without rocking the boat too much, so this is the perfect choice if you get a little shaky on the water. There are several excellent sailing areas around Turkey, with the southern coast being the most popular. Whether you're sailing on the Mediterranean or the Aegean, you're going to find more coves, beaches, bays, and inlets than you can even begin to count. One of the sailing hot spots is the Carian coast between Bodrum and Marmaris. The scenery you'll find here is spectacular, so don't forget to bring your camera and binoculars.

Some other top sailing spots include:
- Antayla
- Bodrum
- Kekova
- Kas
- The Gokova Gulf
- The Hisaranu Gulf

One of the first things you'll notice that's different about sailing in Turkey are the boats. In Turkey they call their boats "gulets" and these wooden beauties are a far cry from the typical sleek narrow boats you see in the United States and Europe. Turkish gulets are much wider, and because of this you have more room to roam around, and you don't feel the waves as much. The gulets were originally used by fishermen but now have been overhauled and spiffed up to fit into Turkey's growing sailing industry.

One of the best words to describe sailing in Turkey is "peaceful." This is not a sailing destination full of fancy casinos and bling. When you're sailing along Turkey's historic coastline you can stop and explore quaint local villages where the people couldn't be friendlier. Visiting Turkey is like stepping back in time because you're surrounded by archaeological sites and medieval architecture. Other exciting areas to explore around Turkey include the Ionian Coast and both the western and eastern Lycian Coast.

 DESTINATION: *New York*

If you're looking to stay a little closer to home, a surprising TRAVEL THERAPY sailing destination is right outside of New York City. Who would have thought? The Northeast is a smart choice if you're limited on time but still want to get out on the water and enjoy the sailing experience. To beat the chilly winter temperatures, the sailing season runs from April through October, with the warmer summer months being the most popular. If you're a novice and are starting to panic about sailing out in the Atlantic Ocean, don't worry—there are plenty of "calmer" sailing options inside the protected Long Island Sound and right on the Hudson River.

One of the things I like best about this sailing location, besides its convenience, is that it's a fantastic place to learn to sail. If you've ever wanted to try navigating your own boat, this is the place to come.

When you're shopping around for sailing schools make sure to find a school that has a strong reputation. For decades one of the top choices for lessons has been the Offshore Sailing School (www.offshore -sailing.com) with locations at Chelsea Piers in Manhattan, Liberty Landing in New Jersey, and Chesapeake Bay in Maryland. This prestigious sailing school was founded in 1964 by America's Cup sailor and Olympic competitor Steve Colgate, and you can either sign

up for the three-day Learn to Sail program or just go for a two-hour mini-lesson to see how you like it. Prices are reasonable, but be sure to book ahead so you can find the class that fits what you're looking for.

If you're searching for a more Jimmy Buffett-type sailing experience, the Offshore Sailing School also offers classes at several locations in Florida and the British Virgin Islands.

▲ *Offshore Sailing School/ New York City*
© OFFSHORE SAILING SCHOOL

DESTINATION: *The Grenadines*

If your idea of a sailing vacation includes warm tropical breezes and sugary sand beaches, DO NOT PASS GO. Head directly to the Grenadines! This inspiring TRAVEL THERAPY destination is the first place I ever spent an entire week on a sailboat. This trip gave me a true taste of what the sailing experience is all about and I've been addicted ever since.

What makes the Grenadines so special? They are a collection of more than thirty Caribbean islands about ninety miles west of Barbados, and only a handful of them are in-habited. This area of the Caribbean makes a fantastic sailing destination because the trade winds never disappoint, and many of the top islands are so close together that you can eas-ily sail from one to another. Since there is so much to see and experience in the Grenadines, it's a good idea to do some research before you go to decide which islands you want to visit so you don't miss anything. This way you'll have a tentative route mapped out and won't be overwhelmed when you get there. Keep in mind, though, that one of the best parts about sailing is changing your course at a moment's notice if the mood strikes you.

One great resource for finding out more about the Grenadines is www.grenadines .net. You can spend hours on this website surfing through all the information. Some of my favorite islands include: Palm Island, St. Vincent, Petit St. Vincent, Bequia, Carriacou, Tobago Cays, Mayreau, and Union Island.

It won't take you long to learn that each island has its own distinct personality. For example, Palm Island is a tiny exclusive pri-vate island where you'll find only one resort. St. Vincent has a bustling Caribbean com-munity where you can find some cute shops, walking tours, and one of the oldest botanical gardens in the Western Hemisphere. Bequia is known for its charm and its adorable, col-orful gingerbread homes; Carriacou is a quiet beach escape; and the Tobago Cays are fa-mous for diving and snorkeling. One of the best-kept secrets in the Grenadines is the tiny island of Mayreau, where only a few hundred people live in one quaint little vil-lage. No matter what you're looking for, if it's a romantic private island escape or a little piece of Caribbean history and culture, the Grenadines deliver.

HOUDINI VACATIONS
Quick Weekend Escapes

How many times in your life have you wanted to get away with your loved one but you were both too busy? You knew there was no way to run off to a tropical island for a week, but how about for a weekend? Too many couples think they don't have the time or money for a weeklong vacation, so they don't go away at all. The solution is a TRAVEL THERAPY Houdini Vacation where you can pack all kinds of romance into forty-eight hours if you pick the right destination. It's amazing how the right mini-vacation can revitalize your relationship, and there are some fantastic places you can visit where you don't have to spend all your time on a plane and still be transported to a romantic destination that feels special and different. The trick is to not just run off to any destination, figuring as long as you get away you'll be fine. Not true! Getting away is great, but if you pick the wrong destination you'll just end up bitter and disappointed because your time is so precious and now you've just wasted it and your money at a crappy resort that doesn't even begin to feel romantic.

When you have limited time together, atmosphere is everything. Go with the mind frame that this weekend is just for the two of you and the goal is romance. Don't be tempted to spend the whole weekend calling your friends on the phone or catching up on your email. A Houdini Vacation can be magical if you play your cards right.

 DESTINATION: *Cabo San Lucas, Mexico*

If you live on the West Coast, Cabo San Lucas, on the tip of the Baja Peninsula, is *the* place to travel to in Mexico because you can leave your home in the morning and be on the beach in Cabo sipping an umbrella drink in time for lunch. The trip from Los Angeles, Phoenix, and San Diego is only about two hours, and convenience is key when the clock is ticking. Besides convenience, Cabo also has some of the most romantic resorts south of the border. Notoriously busy Hollywood A-listers discovered Cabo years ago, so the destination knows how to cater to the luxury crowd and the top resorts specialize in making even a short stay sizzle.

The main downtown area of Cabo San Lucas is filled with colorful tiny shops, restaurants, and bars that are always fun to visit, but for your romantic escape, you'll want to head to one of the ultra-exclusive resorts just outside the city where the emphasis is peace and quiet and superb service. One of the original romantic getaways is the One&Only Palmilla (www.oneandonly palmilla.com), founded in 1956 by Don Abelardo Rodrigues, who is often credited with starting the tourism movement in the Los Cabos area. From Hemingway to Harlow, Hollywood stars have been staying at this first-class resort for decades. What I love about this resort is that it feels small and intimate, despite its 172 rooms. This is one of the few places in the world where I've walked into one of the oceanfront suites and thought, *I could live here, easily!* The daybeds you'll find on your private terrace are the perfect place to sip a nightcap or toast the sunrise.

Another ultra-romantic resort is Las Ventanas al Paraiso (www.lasventanas.com), a favorite with honeymooners and couples who are looking for that truly exclusive and private experience. This secluded hotel has sixty-one beautifully decorated rooms and the feel is posh without being pretentious. You almost feel like you want to whisper so you don't break the spell of this magical destination. As with most top hotels, if you're looking to stay at a specific time you'll want to book early because a paradise like this is very popular.

Learn more about the area by checking out the Los Cabos Tourism Board's website at www.visitloscabos.org.

"I lived in Arizona, so Mexico was the perfect pick for a quick last-minute getaway with my boyfriend because we didn't have to spend all our time traveling. It was a chance for us to be together without having to hang out with our friends. It was great to explore something new together as a couple."

—Carolyn Carver, Television Reporter, Phoenix, Arizona

◀ *View from One&Only Palmilla Resort, Cabo San Lucas, Mexico*
© KAREN SCHALER

DESTINATION: *Bermuda*

Just a hop, skip, and a jump from the East Coast, Bermuda is a beautiful tropical playground that's easily accessible but still has the feel of a remote romantic retreat. The first thing I noticed when I arrived was the sugary pink beaches. Sure, I had heard about the sand being pink in Bermuda, but I never really expected it to be that pink!

So what makes it this color? The locals like to say that it comes from ground-up corals and seashells, but scientists say it's more likely the result of a single-cell marine animal whose red skull gets crushed up along with white seashells to give the sand its pinkish color. Either way, the beaches in Bermuda are breathtaking.

When you're visiting here, don't even think about calling Bermuda part of the Caribbean because the locals will quickly correct you. If you look on the map, Bermuda is very far away from the Caribbean Islands, and Bermudians are very proud of this fact. They're also proud of how clean their island is. In Bermuda you won't find any tacky billboards, litter, graffiti, or racy topless beaches. The people of Bermuda are well educated and there's almost no illiteracy.

To learn more about the history of Bermuda and about specific areas of the island to explore, a good starting point is the Bermuda Department of Tourism website at www .bermudatourism.com. From luxurious large resorts to cute bed-and-breakfasts, you have your pick of accommodations when you stay in Bermuda. To cut down on crazy tourist traffic there are no rental cars allowed on the island, but it's easy to get a taxi whenever you need one.

Bermuda has a reputation for having some of the friendliest people you'll ever find, and on my trips there I've always found this to be true. What makes Bermuda such a successful TRAVEL THERAPY destination is its interesting mixture of different cultural influences. Bermuda is a British colony where the people love cricket, but you'll also find touches of African music and art throughout the island. It is the kind of quick escape where you feel like you've traveled far away from the United States, and yet from the East Coast it's only a two-hour flight away. This gives you more time to do the things you want as a couple, and that alone is precious.

▶ *Pink Sand Beaches at the Fairmont Southampton Resort, Bermuda*
© THE FAIRMONT SOUTHAMPTON, BERMUDA

DESTINATION: *Bal Harbour, Florida*

Bal Harbour is a little slice of luxury tucked away on the very tip of the barrier island most people know as Miami Beach. Nestled between Miami, Fort Lauderdale, and South Beach, Bal Harbour is known as an elite "village" that's overflowing with first-class designer shops, restaurant, spas, and hotels. Believe it or not, you'll find all of this in just one square mile, making it the perfect place to leave your car in the garage so you can get out and do some walking.

There's a certain charm in Bal Harbour that's contagious, and you'll find yourself relaxing almost immediately. You can do as little or as much as you want to, and even though you have some of the most amazing shops and restaurants at your fingertips, the mood is still subdued and laid-back.

For a romantic place to stay the top choice is The Regent Bal Harbour, which opened in 2008. The Regent is the first new hotel built in Bal Harbour in more than fifty years and it was absolutely worth the wait. Besides the 124 designer rooms, a world-class art collection, a sensational spa, and cuisine to die for, you'll find many little extras here that make this property unique and extraordinary. During your stay you're made to feel like an honored guest and part of the family. One very cool amenity and a TRAVEL THERAPY first are the "toe testers" in the showers that allow you to test the water temperature with your toe before taking the plunge. Now that's something different!

For the ultimate in privacy many of the rooms have their own elevator. If you want to surprise your loved one and wear something new to dinner, but don't feel like shopping, The Regent even has a personal shopper standing by to make sure you look fabulous. This property specializes in personalized service, so if there's something you need to make your romantic weekend even more special, don't hesitate to ask.

AUTHOR'S PICK

DESTINATION: *British Virgin Islands*

Of all the romantic vacations I've taken, I have to say sailing in the British Virgin Islands (BVI) is top on my list of things to do when I really want to get away and spend quality time with someone. The first time I looked at exploring this part of the world I never thought it was something I could afford. It was back in the late 1990s and I was researching some resorts in the BVI, looking for the best place to spend a romantic week with my then boyfriend. I had narrowed my choice down to three resorts but couldn't decide. That's when a friend suggested we charter a sailboat, check out all the islands, and then come back the following year to stay a week on the island we liked the most. I remember thinking, *Sure, if I win the lottery.* Still, the idea intrigued me enough that I started snooping around to see what it would cost and was amazed to find that if you planned your trip right, it was no more than what it would cost to stay at an average resort in the United States.

If you have no idea how to sail, don't worry—you can also hire a captain. It's a lot easier than you might think if you go through a group like The Moorings (www .moorings.com) that specializes in charter

trips like this. You get to pick your food and drinks ahead of time and when you arrive at the starting point in Tortola, after a short briefing, you're sent off to find your boat, meet the captain, and put away your supplies.

For my first sailing trip, to keep costs down, we picked a small sailboat that was perfect for just the two of us—and our captain. For my second trip several years later, we upgraded to a larger catamaran. While it was nice having all the extra space, the truth is it was more romantic having the smaller sailboat. Some people have asked me, "How romantic can it be if you have a captain on the boat with you?" A common concern, but on both of my trips I found the captains to be extremely sensitive to our privacy. Every night when we were relaxing on the boat the captain would take the dinghy and go ashore to the nearest island and not come back until well after we were asleep. If we wanted to hang out on the island then the captain would stay on the boat. It was the perfect setup.

I love the BVI for a TRAVEL THERAPY destination because it has some of the most beautiful water in the Caribbean. The snorkeling is outstanding and the islands you sail around feature some of the most amazing

resorts in the world. These are not the kinds of islands where you'll find a lot of people and touristy shops. These are tiny specs of civilization where the emphasis is on relaxation and sometimes the only thing on the island is one resort. On that first sailing trip, my boyfriend and I spent every night on the boat, while on the second trip we alternated between staying on the boat and staying at a resort. It cost a lot more to go ashore but it was worth every penny.

If you're going to splurge, top islands to stay at include: Peter Island, Virgin Gorda, Scrub Island, Necker Island, Guana Island, and Tortola. To help you decide what islands you might want to visit, check out this information-packed website: www.british virginislands.com.

"When I learned to sail as a young adult, my life changed forever. I discovered the sheer joy of taking the helm and handling the lines while seeing the world under sail. Cruising on a sailboat is an eco-friendly way to travel that utterly (and literally) takes one to distant ports and tiny islands no cruise ships would dare visit. In a world of 24/7 news and wireless transmissions, traveling under sail stops the clock, gently and long enough to refresh one's soul."

—DORIS COLGATE, CEO, OFFSHORE SAILING SCHOOL, WORLDWIDE

Ready For Romance Vacation Checklist

CHOOSE TRIPS WHERE YOU CAN:

- Reconnect
- Bond
- Relax
- Find romance
- Sizzle
- Escape

◀ *Sailing in the British Virgin Islands*
© KAREN SCHALER

"Travel is fatal to prejudice, bigotry, and narrow-mindedness, and many of our people need it sorely on these accounts. Broad, wholesome, charitable views of men and things cannot be acquired by vegetating in one little corner of the earth all one's lifetime."

—MARK TWAIN

Chapter 4

Pay It Forward

*I*f you're looking at your life and feeling like there's something missing, and you just know in your gut there's so much more you could do, so much more you could contribute, then a volunteer vacation might be just what you need to get on the right track to Pay It Forward. We all know how easy it is to get caught up in our own stress. We end up shutting out the rest of the world. You figure you're having a hard enough time dealing with your own issues, so there's no way you can deal with all the other problems going on around you. Ironically, living in your own bubble can backfire, making you feel even more isolated and alone. Taking off your protective blinders and getting involved in what's happening to other people—and doing something to help—can be empowering beyond belief. The choice to Pay It Forward is yours and yours alone. When you are ready, here are three different TRAVEL THERAPY options:

- If You Build It—Construction Volunteer Projects
- Sharing Your Heart—Volunteering with Children
- Resorting to Help—Going Green

If you need help picking the trip that's right for you, just take this simple TRAVEL THERAPY quiz to get you on your way.

◀ *Children at Njobvu Cultural Village in Malawi, Africa*
© KAREN SCHALER

TRAVEL THERAPY QUIZ

1. You would rather:
   a. Build something
   b. Play with kids
   c. Recycle

2. You are more skilled at:
   a. Slinging a hammer
   b. Reading to children
   c. Tending to plants and animals

3. You would rather buy:
   a. A tool kit
   b. Toys
   c. Hiking boots

4. Your preferred store is:
   a. The Home Depot
   b. Toys "R" Us
   c. Eddie Bauer

5. What sounds best?
   a. A weeklong building project
   b. A week with kids
   c. A week enjoying the environment

6. You like working most with:
   a. Adults
   b. Children
   c. Nature

7. The most appealing projects are when:
   a. You can physically see the outcome
   b. There's an emotional payback
   c. What you've done doesn't leave a huge carbon footprint

TRAVEL THERAPY DIAGNOSIS

If you have mostly "A" answers, then check out a volunteer vacation under If You Build It because these trips involve physical labor where you can take pride in the finished product. If "B" is your answer of choice, then go for a trip under Sharing Your Heart, where working with children will help feed your spirit. Finally, if the majority of your answers are "C," then you'll want to explore the Resorting to Help section to find a "green" volunteer experience where you can connect with the environment.

DESTINATIONS TO AVOID:

- Superficial destinations
- Self-absorbed destinations
- Places that are flashy and without substance
- Spots that are only good to brag about
- Phony destinations
- Places that are ridiculously expensive for no real reason

"As a clinical psychologist, I have taught psychotherapy to professionals in forty different countries and I have visited numerous other countries. I learned more about life and living life meaningfully by traveling then I did in all my years of formal education."

—JEFFREY K. ZEIG, PhD, DIRECTOR OF THE
MILTON H. ERICKSON FOUNDATION, PHOENIX, ARIZONA

IF YOU BUILD IT
Construction Volunteer Projects

If your motto is "have hammer, will travel," then a volunteer vacation where the goal is building something that's needed—like a school or home—is the perfect opportunity for you to get involved in a construction project that can literally change lives. There's always pride in making something from scratch, but when your building project also helps provide a home for a family or a school for a child, then the payback is tenfold!

If you love the idea of volunteering for a building project but you've never swung a hammer before, don't worry—there are still plenty of ways you can contribute. There's always room on these types of volunteer trips for an eager beginner who's open to learning new skills and willing to help out with whatever is needed. Just remember, not everyone has to know the difference between a Phillips-head screwdriver and that other one. Just because you're not a whiz with the drill or don't know how to drywall doesn't mean there's not plenty you can do to help move the project along. If, on the other hand, you do know what you're doing, and even have your own handy tool belt, more power to you!

 DESTINATION: *Habitat for Humanity, Worldwide*

"If you build it, they will come." Okay, so that line from the movie *Field of Dreams* is actually talking about building a baseball field, but the idea is basically the same. If something is built that people want and need, they will come. And where volunteer destinations are concerned, the people are already there, eagerly waiting for their new home or school.

When you think about volunteer trips that involve building things, the first organization that usually comes to mind is Habitat for Humanity International. Founded in 1976 by Millard Fuller and his wife, Linda, Habitat for Humanity offers a long list of projects that span the globe, with programs in more than ninety countries. Since its inception, Habitat for Humanity has built more than 250,000 homes in more than three thousand different communities, providing more than one million people a place to call home. This nonprofit organization is known for reacting to current needs after natural disasters like

hurricanes, tornadoes, and tsunamis. The list of projects is always changing, so if you're interested in participating in a Habitat for Humanity volunteer program, your best bet is to go to the organization's website at www.habitat.org and research the different volunteer opportunities available.

Some standout projects include the ongoing Thailand Tsunami-Reconstruction Program, the Youth Programs, the Global Village Program, and the unique Women Build Program, where women from all over the world get together to pool their skills and resources to focus on different construction projects. This all-women's building program empowers not only the women who are doing the building, but also the women in the community who are watching their homes being built by smart, talented, and capable women.

▲ *Habitat for Humanity Volunteers at a Habitat Women Build in Jordan.*
© HABITAT FOR HUMANITY/DAVID SNYDER

Probably one of Habitat for Humanity's most well-known projects is the Carter Work Project, which started in 1984 when former President Jimmy Carter and his wife Rosalynn led a work group in New York City to help renovate a building for nineteen families who needed affordable housing. Now each year Jimmy and Rosalynn give a week of their time and energy to help build homes with volunteers from around the world. The goal, aside from completing the much-needed homes, is to gain more awareness and attention for the growing need for more affordable housing.

Habitat for Humanity's longevity means it has a strong track record for paying it forward. When I asked David Minich, director of volunteer logistics, why people looking for a volunteer trip should consider Habitat for Humanity, he told me, "Travelers choose to join Habitat for Humanity building teams for many reasons. Some people feel a significant need to give back to the world, some have a deep desire to do something specific to show their care and concern for others, and some are passionate about the idea of affordable housing around the world. Habitat for Humanity's Global Village Program is designed to offer a structure for individuals who want to pour a little sweat into their travel plans."

No matter what your reason for wanting to volunteer, the key is actually getting out there and doing it, taking a stand, and making a difference one nail, one screwdriver, and one hammer at a time.

 DESTINATION: *Guatemala*

If you don't have time to travel halfway around the world for a volunteer vacation but you still want to get out of the country and experience a different culture, a great volunteer group called Ambassadors for Children (AFC), based in the United States, offers a fantastic and affordable one-week trip to Guatemala. This trip's focus is on light construction work and interacting with poverty-stricken children in the La Esquintla region of Guatemala.

When I was researching volunteer vacations, I chose AFC for my first trip not only for its affordability, but also because it builds an itinerary for you to volunteer where it's most needed while getting a chance to do some exploring around the area. With all AFC trips you will be working and sightseeing, so you will have an opportunity to absorb some of the culture and gain a better understanding of the people you are helping.

◀ *Habitat for Humanity's Women Build Program*
© HABITAT FOR HUMANITY/KIM MACDONALD

Ambassadors for Children (www.ambassadorsforchildren.org) was founded in 1998 and has offered hundreds of humanitarian trips around the world, donating more than five million dollars in aid and helping children in twenty different countries. Another bonus of going on a trip with AFC is that the organization is known for picking out-of-the-way, remote destinations that aren't always in the limelight, so you feel like you're making a difference in a part of the world that doesn't always get a lot of attention.

For the one-week Guatemala program, AFC partners with the Vamos Adelante Foundation and the Open Windows Foundation, which support schools and literacy projects in the Esquintla region, an area that includes eighteen villages. The AFC credo sums it up best:

Grateful for the opportunity to experience the world and serve children as a global volunteer and because peace begins with the individual, I affirm my personal responsibility and commitment to:

- Journey with an open mind and a gentle heart.

- Accept with grace and gratitude the diversity I encounter.

- Revere and protect the natural environment, which sustains all life.

- Appreciate all cultures I discover.

- Respect and thank my hosts for their welcome.

- Offer my hand in friendship to everyone I meet.

- Support services that share these views and act upon them and,

- By my spirit, words, and actions, encourage others to travel the world in peace.

"My trip to Guatemala gave me a better understanding of the need in so many foreign countries. When I think of all the amenities I have I cannot help to think that so much more can be done to help those in need. Seeing the kids' smiling faces as we worked with them made my heart melt and I believe that everyone should experience this."

—Dana Delany-Anders, Former Guatemala Volunteer, Indiana

THAT'S MY SEAT! *AIRLINE TIPS*

If you choose a volunteer vacation in a foreign country, then you want to be sure to get your plane seat assignment well in advance, or you'll end up at your destination feeling like a pretzel. Trust me, this is no time to get stuck in a cramped middle seat or be wedged in a seat that doesn't recline because the exit row is behind you. (Federal regulations won't let seats in front of an exit row recline.) When I fly, I'll only sit in an aisle seat, especially on long flights, so I can get up and stretch my legs without having to climb over anyone who might be sleeping or blocking my way. Sure, you might get bumped by the food cart occasionally, but it's still better than being packed into the plane like a sardine.

When selecting your seat, be careful not to get a seat next to the bathrooms or you'll never get any rest, especially on an overnight flight with people moving around all night. If you can afford first or business class, this is the time to splurge and spend the money, or use your air miles to upgrade. But if you're stuck in coach like the rest of us, at least try to see if you can score an exit aisle seat because it will give you the most legroom. A fantastic website I always use to check the seat options on a plane is www.seatguru.com. Once you find out the kind of plane you're flying in, like a Boeing 747, you can bring up the seat map and find the best options. The website even color codes good seats and seats to avoid, giving explanations. Checking my seats beforehand on this site has saved me from some serious seating nightmares!

 DESTINATION: *Belize*

In the Central American country of Belize there are a number of different opportunities to volunteer where construction projects are the focus, but you still have a chance to experience the beauty of this coastal country and discover everything from its world-renowned coral reefs to its ancient Mayan ruins. The GoAbroad.com organization (www .goabroad.com) is a great resource when you're researching trips because it allows groups offering different volunteer opportunities to publish their information for free on its website. One of the organization's founders, Troy Peden, says their diversified website includes everything from volunteering at a woman's village co-op in Afghanistan to the Peace Corps.

The website was developed by a group of international educators after they did extensive research about what was need-ed and wanted in a volunteer vacation. GoAbroad.com works with different partners from around the world and offers some truly unique volunteer vacations, including sev-eral programs in Belize. Peden says, "We be-lieve volunteering abroad changes the world by changing the attitudes and experience of individuals."

To volunteer with GoAbroad.com's many partners, you're often required to do a phone interview and submit a written application, which is a fantastic idea, because it weeds out anyone who is not sincerely dedicated to the volunteer experience. To go on a volunteer trip you have to have an open mind and not be too picky about your accommodations. I heard a story about a woman on one trip to a remote region of Africa who ordered wine at dinner and complained because the bottle

didn't have a vintage year on it. She should have been thankful to find any kind of wine available. So be forewarned. Most volunteer trips aren't going to include award-winning wine tasting or culinary experiences. What you will discover instead are delicious local dishes that challenge your taste buds and your imagination.

One of the bonuses about volunteering in Belize where you're building schools or work-ing with school children is knowing that you're doing your part to help a country improve its educational opportunities. To make sure you sign up for a volunteer experience where the goal of the project is what you're looking for, research the website carefully, and even call if you have questions about the itinerary. You don't want to end up traveling all the way there just to find out the trip isn't what you expected and then be disappointed.

SHARING YOUR HEART
Volunteering with Children

You hear people talk about how volunteering in Africa changed their lives, but I didn't truly understand the concept until I signed up for a volunteer vacation to work with children at an orphanage. During this life-changing vol-unteer experience, I quickly learned it's not about how many toys you can give a child but

rather the time you spend with them—really listening to them, hugging them, and laughing with them—that makes the most difference. Working with children who may be troubled, sick, or scared is not for everyone. You have to have an infinite amount of patience and the ability to put a child's needs before your

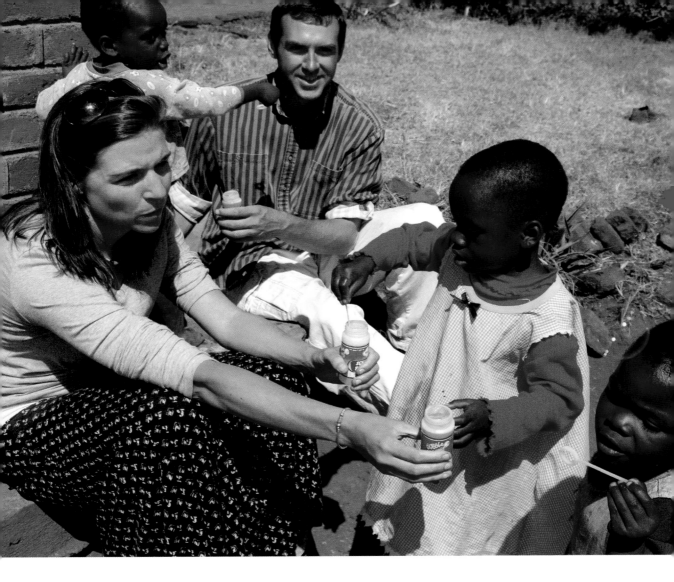

own. Ask yourself before signing up for this kind of trip if you can look at children who may be starving or suffering from HIV/AIDS and still pick them up and hug them. Even more important, can you spend time with these children and open your own heart wide enough to let them in? If the answer is yes, keep reading, because the following volunteer trips that focus on children will break and fill up your heart at the same time. Volunteer trips where you work with children are amazingly powerful, so be prepared to be inspired and moved, and to learn what it really means to Pay It Forward.

▲ *Volunteers Playing with Orphaned Children in Africa*
© KAREN SCHALER

"After the sudden, tragic death of my husband, I was devastated and paralyzed emotionally. I decided to go to Africa to volunteer with my church, having no idea the impact it would have on my life. I learned no matter how hard things could get I could handle it, and that instead of letting a tragedy cripple me I would grow from the experience and learn how to give back at the same time."

—DANA BLANCHARD, VOLUNTEER AT MTENDERE ORPHANAGE, ALABAMA

 DESTINATION: *Africa*

There are dozens of locations around Africa where volunteer vacations are aimed at helping some of the world's neediest children. Whether your volunteer trip takes you to Uganda, Ethiopia, Kenya, South Africa, or Malawi, chances are you're going to meet children who have no one to call family, whose mothers and fathers have died from HIV/AIDS, and who have been abandoned and often abused. The lucky ones, if you can call a child without parents "lucky," will have a home at an orphanage, but the majority of the children in these poverty-stricken countries are left wandering the streets, struggling daily to find food so they don't starve to death. When you volunteer in Africa you are often helping children who are living in desperate circumstances. Seeing how they live and how much they suffer is heartbreaking. This is not supposed to be easy, but helping even one child is what makes it worth it.

The Ambassadors for Children volunteer organization offers several two-week programs throughout Africa where you will work directly with children in an orphanage, a village, a hospital, or all three. There are many programs to choose from, but the general theme is consistent. Your job is to interact with and help the children any way you can. AFC asks that each volunteer bring a bag of donated items with them for the children because getting supplies to most of these countries through regular mail is a huge challenge; it can take months for any mail to arrive, if it arrives at all. To make it simple, AFC gives you a list ahead of time so you know what is most needed. At the end of the volunteer trip all donations are divvied up evenly so each child will receive something special. It's always stressed that no matter what special connection you make with one specific child, you're not allowed to give that child a gift because it wouldn't be fair to the

rest of the group. So if you want to give a child a piece of chocolate, you'd better have enough for everyone.

For AFC's volunteer vacations in Africa, your living arrangements and meals are usually pretty simple because there aren't a lot of lodging and food options in the areas where you're volunteering. AFC's website offers a little tip to get its volunteers in the right frame of mind: "Volunteers are expected to be flexible since this is Africa and things don't always go as planned!" Once you arrive in Africa, you quickly learn to ignore your watch and go with the flow; every time you hit a glitch it's best to just shrug your shoulders and remind yourself: "This is Africa." You can either say it with a grin or grimace. If you're going to enjoy your experience, I highly recommend the grin.

For each trip, AFC has a packet of detailed information you can download from it's website—a huge help when you're trying to select the best volunteer vacation to fit your expectations. Anyone can download the packet, so it's a great resource to have if you're just starting your research. As with many volunteer organizations, when you sign up for an AFC trip you're responsible for getting to the country where you're volunteering on your own. During the program itself, all your transportation to and from different sites is included. The prices for AFC trips vary, but two-week program trips usually run under $2,000. Keep in mind that prices can change quickly depending on what's happening in the country at the time you're planning to go, so be sure to get the latest details from the website so there are no surprises.

▲ *Volunteer at Mtendere Orphanage in Malawi, Africa*
© KAREN SCHALER

 DESTINATION: *India*

If you've always craved an exotic adventure in South Asia, then consider India for one of the most unique TRAVEL THERAPY destinations for a volunteer vacation. A word of warning, though, you'd better not mind crowds because India has the second largest population in the world, with more than one billion people! Unfortunately, inflation, a growing food crisis, and the HIV/AIDS epidemic that has devastated parts of Africa are now taking their toll on India, wreaking havoc on this country's children. As a result,

India is seeing a growing number of orphans, which has in turn meant that various volunteer programs are now partnering with orphanages around the country to try to help these children.

An organization called Parmarth Gurukul, a home for children without parents, houses around one hundred and fifty orphaned boys. The focus here is to make sure these boys get

▲ *Author Karen Schaler volunteering at Malawi Orphanage*
© KAREN SCHALER

a good education so they can become active members in the Indian community. Another group, Ramana's Seva Samiti (Ramana's Garden), is a home for orphaned and impoverished children. Ambassadors for Children offers volunteer programs where you can help at both of these homes and also have the opportunity to experience the culture of the surrounding communities. One unique aspect about AFC's volunteer trip to India is that it includes a trip to Rishikesh, known as the "City of the Divine" and the yoga capital of the world, and a day tour of New Delhi.

Because of India's growing needs, most top volunteer organizations are now putting together trips to India, so depending on your timetable and your objective, you shouldn't have a problem finding a volunteer program in this country. One great resource for tracking down a volunteer organization offering trips where you want to go is www.volunteer abroad.com. This website gives you various links to different volunteer groups from around the world, and it's a good place to start when you're trying to narrow down your options.

 DESTINATION: *Vietnam*

After decades of struggle, there is now light at the end of the tunnel for Vietnam. This battered, war-torn country joined the World Trade Organization in 2007 and is working to increase employment opportunities throughout Vietnam. Though government statistics show that the level of severe poverty is going down, Vietnam is still a country in need where volunteer vacations can make a huge difference.

There are numerous volunteer opportunities around Vietnam, including programs in Hanoi and Ho Chi Minh City (formerly Saigon), where you can teach English, work at an orphanage, volunteer at a hospital, or even care for disabled children. Different

trips offer different living arrangements, but if you're looking for total immersion you can even set up to stay with a local family. One major bonus to this TRAVEL THERAPY destination is that many volunteer programs in Vietnam are quite affordable. I found some starting as low as $500 for two weeks, so be sure to do your research to find the best organization and price possible.

If you're a foodie and searching for a different way to get involved, you can find a unique volunteer program at www.i-to-i.com that literally puts you right in a kitchen. The two-week program is offered in Ho Chi Minh City where you work in a cooking house for the poor. As a volunteer, you'll prepare about two thousand meals a day and deliver them by hand to the needy around the city and in the hospitals.

Vietnam as a volunteer destination is growing in popularity every day, so the list of volunteer opportunities just continues to increase. Your smartest option for finding the latest news and new volunteer offerings is to use a website like www.goabroad.com, where there is plenty of information about volunteer partners offering trips to Vietnam. For these volunteer vacations you can go for as little as two weeks or stay six months or more, depending on what your schedule can accommodate.

RESORTING TO HELP
Going Green

A new trend in volunteerism is selecting a green-friendly program where the focus is on giving back to the environment. Some of the volunteer programs focus on specific animals that might be endangered or threatened, while others concentrate on eco-friendly trips where you deal with issues like the disappearing rainforests and global warming.

DESTINATION: *Thailand*

For this volunteer destination, not only do you get to experience an amazing country that's known for its fascinating scenery and age-old traditions, but you also get to monkey around a little and work with one of Thailand's most interesting creatures, the white-handed gibbon. The focus of this volunteer program is rehabilitating these monkeys so they can be returned to the wild. Learning about how to protect the gibbon's habitat, the rainforest, is also a huge component.

The Gibbon Rehabilitation Project (GRP) in Thailand was set up in 1992 and is now part of the Wild Animal Rescue Foundation (WARF) of Thailand. The project is located at the Bang Pae waterfall in Phuket, Thailand, in the Khao Pra Theaw non-hunting area. Researchers say one of the biggest threats to Thailand's gibbon population is the destruction of where they live as increased tourism and development move into the rainforest. There's also the growing problem of people catching gibbons and keeping them as pets, or selling them in the illegal pet trade. The GRP is working to educate people about the gibbons and to stop the illegal use and exploitation of these monkeys. Sadly, there have even been reports of the animals being captured and used for entertainment in bars, where the gibbons are forced to smoke cigarettes and drink alcohol.

If this is a volunteer program that sparks your interest, here's what you can expect. Volunteers with the GRP will have a number of different opportunities to interact with the animals. Over the course of the project, volunteers research the animals, help prepare their food, and learn how to feed them by using baskets that hang from a pull rope. Probably the most satisfying part of this volunteer program is when the gibbons are released back into the rainforest. The releases are carefully set up so that the volunteers can still chart the monkeys' movements and eating patterns after they're let go.

Thailand means "land of the free," and this is one Travel Therapy destination that's all about freedom for the gibbons and making sure this part of Thailand's legacy lives on forever.

 DESTINATION: *Peru*

Usually when you think of traveling to Peru, the famous Machu Picchu comes to mind—it is, after all, the country's number one tourist attraction. Hiking this ancient peak is a fantastic Travel Therapy trip, but if you're looking for a way to give back to the environment and help conserve the local landscape, you'll want to check out one of the many eco-tour programs going on in Peru. A great resource to find different green-friendly trips in Peru (and beyond) is an organization called ProWorld Service Corps (www.my proworld.org).

Adam Saks of ProWorld says that volunteers with this nonprofit organization work with host communities in Peru, Belize, Mexico, India, and Thailand to help save their natural resources for future generations. "Our volunteers have planted more than ten thousand native plants and trees, built over fifteen hundred cleaner burning stoves, and educated hundreds of children about environmental conservation," says Saks.

One program on the site has volunteers training locals in Peru to be tour guides in the Sacred Valley of the Incas, teaching them everything from customer service to the history of the area. The motivation behind this is to educate these new guides so that they can in turn offer their own eco-tours and educate visitors about the native plants and different environmental issues that are important to preserving Peru's natural resources.

Another program, the Clean Burning Stove Project, has volunteers teaching native Peruvians safer ways to cook their meals so they aren't polluting their own environment and breathing unhealthy air. Right now most people in the rural area of Urubamba cook indoors over an open fire with barely any ventilation. In the Clean Burning Stove Project, volunteers work to install fuel-efficient wood stoves in homes with the hopes of creating a healthier environment and protecting the Sacred Valley's endangered forests.

As green programs gain even more popularity, expect to find a growing number of volunteer programs in Peru. Projects will vary throughout the year, so if you don't find something right away that jumps out at you, keep looking, because chances are the Pay It Forward trip you're looking for is just around the corner.

 DESTINATION: *Colorado*

If you're craving a Pay It Forward vacation, but you're on a serious budget, or if you'd rather do your part closer to home, there are some fabulous volunteer groups that concentrate on green volunteer vacations right here in the United States. One great resource to look into is a group called Wilderness Volunteers (www.wildernessvolunteers.org). This website is quick and easy to use. Just click on the part of the country where you to want volunteer and see what options are available. Another plus: These trips are affordable, costing less than $300 for a week!

One TRAVEL THERAPY destination that stands out for its green volunteer trip options is Colorado. The Rocky Mountain state is one of my favorite winter destinations, so volunteering there when there's no snow on the ground feels almost like a thank-you to Colorado for being such a beautiful winter wonderland. Of course, Colorado is also a world-class summer playground for people who love to go boating, hiking, fishing, and camping, so any way you look at it, it's a win-win situation when it comes to giving back.

One popular area for volunteer work in Colorado is Four Pass Loop, a trail that goes over four different mountain peaks. Wilderness Volunteers trips usually last about a week and combine trail beautification projects with time off so you can enjoy the sensational surroundings and scenery. These Wilderness Volunteers vacations are a great choice if you love camping because you'll be sleeping in a tent all week, which is one of the reasons why prices for these trips are so low. Many of these volunteer vacations also involve a lot of hiking so you need to be in shape, have a comfy backpack, and have your hiking boots ready to rock 'n' roll.

> *"My volunteer vacation to Africa changed my life and my family's life. I went on the trip alone leaving my husband and two young children at home and returned in two weeks a better wife, mother, and friend. I was filled up from the amazing experience and refreshed and ready to be a mom again, only this time I paid more attention to my kids and what was really important in life. . . . "*
>
> —ERIN HEMPEN, MOTHER OF TWO, TRENTON, ILLINOIS

AUTHOR'S PICK

DESTINATION: *Malawi, Africa*

For years I had wanted to volunteer in a remote part of the world but figured I'd need to have a serious amount of cash and unlimited time to travel. I've always had the kind of job where I was never given more than five days off at a time and funds were often tight, so this one travel dream seemed impossible until I quit my job and started living off of my savings. Financially, it was absolutely the worst time to do a volunteer vacation, but something was pushing me forward. When I started researching trips and heard about a new volunteer program in Malawi, Africa,

it was like *BAM!*—Malawi was it. I just knew that was where I was supposed to go, and from that moment on nothing was going to stop me.

I was drawn to the fact that Malawi is one of Africa's poorest countries. A catastrophic number of HIV/AIDS cases have turned Malawi into a country of more than one million orphans. I just felt in my heart if any country needed the help of volunteers it was Malawi.

After some research, I signed up for a two-week volunteer program with Ambassadors

for Children. I had to figure out a way to get to Malawi, because AFC requires that you get to the volunteer destination on your own. AFC caught my eye because it offers a unique way to volunteer in Malawi, where part of your time is spent at the Mtendere Orphanage working with close to one hundred and fifty children, and part of your time includes traveling with your volunteer group around Malawi, learning about the impoverished country by visiting villages, staying in a national park, and being part of a food distribution project. After talking with AFC's founder, Dr. Sally Brown, I knew this was the kind of volunteer organization I was looking for. Brown is passionate about helping children around the world and told me, "Voluntourism allows for a cultural immersion that wouldn't occur by simply going on vacation. It creates bonding with family and camaraderie with other participants like no other vacation would."

My volunteer trip had sixteen participants who had come from all walks of life. There were volunteers from the United States, Mexico, and Holland. In our group we had a stay-at-home mom, an ER nurse, four teenagers, several single people, and even an

▲ *Two Mothers Waiting for a Food Distribution, Africa*
© KAREN SCHALER

Olympian. We couldn't have been more different, but for those two weeks we all came together as a group to help the orphans at Mtendere Village who so desperately needed our love and attention.

The Travel Therapy aspect of this journey is ongoing. The images of Malawi are never far from my mind and I think about the children at the orphanage every day. The orphans I met had lost everything, but the entire time I was there I never saw one child complain. Instead, the children would burst into huge smiles every time they saw us. It took so little to make these children happy. Malawi is where I learned that you don't need to give a child a lot of expensive "things"—all they really need is for someone to spend time with them so they know someone cares and believes in them.

It was hard leaving Malawi, and even more difficult coming back to the States. Life in Malawi was very simple. The children at the orphanage didn't have electricity or hot water, so I felt almost guilty going back to my "regular" life where I have so many things that most of us take for granted. For the first several weeks back home, the members in my volunteer group emailed back and forth creating an informal support group. We all vowed to work on different projects to help "our" Malawi children. We knew that the connections we made with the people of Malawi and one another would last a lifetime. The only negative I could find about doing a volunteer vacation is that one trip isn't enough, because once you get a feel for this kind of Travel Therapy, you'll want to experience it over and over again.

Pay It Forward Vacation Checklist

CHOOSE TRIPS WHERE YOU CAN:

- Give back
- Volunteer
- Be inspired
- Be challenged
- Learn about a new culture
- Help another person

"The most important trip you may take in life is meeting people halfway."

—HENRY BOYE

Chapter 5

Reconnecting

*I*f we're honest, we're all guilty of it: Getting so wrapped up in our own lives, trying not to fall off the merry-go-round of life, that at some time or another we end up losing sight of what matters most. How many times have you heard yourself promise that you'll take a break and go on a vacation with a loved one, or go visit a family member, only to put those plans on the back burner when something more "pressing" came up? It's all about priorities and realizing that if you don't take the time to reconnect with the people who really matter in your life then they might not be there the next time you're ready to fit them into your hectic schedule. Or maybe your loved ones aren't making time for you. Regardless of why this disconnect is happening, Reconnecting TRAVEL THERAPY vacations are all about taking a special vacation where the focus is on spending quality time with the people you care about.

For this TRAVEL THERAPY, selecting the right destination makes all the difference in the world, so here are three smart options to help you on your way:

- A Family Affair—Family-Friendly Vacations
- Roughing It Together—Camping Adventures
- One and Only—Escape for Couples

How do you decide? Take the TRAVEL THERAPY quiz to help you pick the trip that's best for you.

◀ *Sunset Snowshoeing at Northstar-at-Tahoe Resort*
© NORTHSTAR-AT-TAHOE RESORT

TRAVEL THERAPY QUIZ

1. You're looking to travel with:
   a. Your kids
   b. Your kids, relatives, or significant other
   c. Just your significant other

2. Your idea of "roughing it" includes:
   a. Vacationing with kids
   b. Sleeping in a tent
   c. Having only one glass of wine with dinner

3. Your favorite movie is:
   a. Home Alone
   b. Legends of the Fall
   c. Sideways

4. You like staying at:
   a. An affordable hotel
   b. A campground
   c. A luxury resort

5. A great trip includes:
   a. Family-friendly activities
   b. A campfire
   c. Happy Hour

6. You are ready:
   a. For a family adventure
   b. To explore the wilderness
   c. To relax and unwind with no kids

7. Your favorite song is:
   a. "We Are Family"
   b. "Rocky Mountain High"
   c. "Red Red Wine"

8. You'd rather do:
   a. Activities for all ages
   b. Activities outside
   c. Adult-only activities

9. You would rather visit:
   a. A family beach
   b. A campground beach
   c. A luxurious beach

10. When you hear a screaming child you:
    a. Smile—it's probably yours
    b. Worry about noise pollution
    c. Run for the hills

TRAVEL THERAPY DIAGNOSIS

If "A" is the answer you ended up picking the most, then it's time to round up the kids and check out a TRAVEL THERAPY destination under A Family Affair, where the focus is on family-friendly destinations where you can bond and have a great time. If "B" is your answer of choice, then you'll want to grab your hiking boots and granola and check out a camping trip under Roughing It Together. If most of your answers are under the "C" category, then it's time for you and your significant other to take a vacation under the One and Only list, where you can spend some romantic time together remembering why you're with this person in the first place.

DESTINATIONS TO AVOID:

- Work-related destinations
- Places where you're answering work calls
- Places where you're on the computer
- Places where your BlackBerry works
- Places where you're likely to get distracted
- Destinations that you can leave easily
- Places where you're stressed out

"Travel is a magical catalyst for personal transformation. A new environment awakens all the senses of sight, smell, hearing, taste, and touch, forcing one to become present to the moment. This presence revitalizes the soul to see new possibilities and return home with renewed vitality."

—ALLISON CABRAL, CERTIFIED LIFE COACH, ARIZONA

A FAMILY AFFAIR
Family-Friendly Vacations

Of course you love your kids, but have you ever found yourself on a vacation wondering, *What in the world was I thinking bringing these little rascals here?* Your trip ends up being more about surviving the wrong destination than it does about enjoying time together. When you're traveling with children, unless you want to go bonkers, it's absolutely imperative that you do your research and not only pick a place that's child-friendly, but choose a spot that you can enjoy as well, so you all have the vacation that's needed.

This is where TRAVEL THERAPY can come to your rescue. One of the biggest mistakes you can make when traveling with kids is going to a destination that you used to visit before you had kids, but never noticed how completely impractical it is for children. You end up at your beloved vacation spot bewildered and disappointed and ready to pull your hair out. This is not the way you want to spend precious time with your family, so check out the following TRAVEL THERAPY options where both you and your kids can have a special trip you'll always remember.

 DESTINATION: *Lake Tahoe, California/Nevada*

What I love about Lake Tahoe as a TRAVEL THERAPY destination, besides the breathtaking scenery, is how affordable it can be, depending on the kind of family vacation you want to take. You can stick to a budget and still feel like you've splurged because there's so much to do at Lake Tahoe that's absolutely free! You have to love that! Another bonus is that you'll find sunny days at Lake Tahoe more than 75 percent of the year.

Let's start off by looking at why Lake Tahoe is such an ideal TRAVEL THERAPY pick. The lake is actually located in both California and Nevada, and when it comes to size, it's the biggest Alpine lake in North America. There are plenty of places to stay and a long list of things to do at locations all around the lake.

▶ *Skiing at Lake Tahoe*
© SIERRA AT TAHOE RESORT/CHIP ALLEN

Because we are talking about such a large area, the best thing to do is to go to the Lake Tahoe Visitor Bureau website (www.visiting laketahoe.com), so you can do some pre-liminary research before you set off on your journey. A word of advice: Plan to spend at least an hour on this site because there's so much useful information here—and the photos are fantastic! A good way to start out is by narrowing down the time of year you want to visit and where on the lake you want to stay.

Lake Tahoe is separated into north-ern and southern parts. Depending on what you're looking for as a family, both areas offer some great choices.

If you want to bundle up and hit this des-tination in the winter, Lake Tahoe is home to more than a dozen ski resorts, including popular picks like Heavenly Mountain Resort and Squaw Valley, host of the 1960 Winter Olympics.

Once the snow melts and the tempera-tures start to rise, Lake Tahoe is also an im-pressive summer destination with dozens of different hiking and mountain biking trails that are free and open to the public. To find out more, you can go online to download dif-ferent maps of the areas you're interested in.

Water sports are also a popular pick if you want to spend time on the lake. And you can easily spend a week sampling all the different restaurants that you can boat right up to.

Because the lake is so huge, the best plan for a family trip is to select one family-friendly area to call home base. The Northstar Resort area (www.northstarattahoe.com) on the north shore of Lake Tahoe is consistent-ly ranked top in the country for catering to families, and there's so much to do at this impressive destination that you might end up spending your entire vacation here. This year-round mountain resort offers everything from budget hotels and family condos to lux-urious five-bedroom homes, so you can pick the accommodation that matches your bud-get. When you stay in the Northstar Resort area, you have free access to all kinds of recreational activities, ranging from outdoor spas and swimming pools to more than one hundred miles of mountain biking trails. In the summer, Northstar also offers free sce-nic chairlift rides to help get you off on the right foot for your hiking adventure. Insider tip: Book your stay at this part of Lake Tahoe early, because even though there are many different family-friendly accommodations, the best ones fill up fast!

DESTINATION: *Alberta, Canada*

Alberta is one of Canada's most beautiful provinces, and two of my favorite TRAVEL THERAPY destinations in the Canadian Rockies are Banff and Lake Louise. There's a reason why more than one hundred films, including *Brokeback Mountain* and *Legends of the Fall,* have been filmed in Alberta. This part of the world has some of the most spectacular scenery I've ever seen.

You can visit this destination year-round, but in the dead of winter the freezing temperatures can really take a bite out of your vacation plans, especially when you're traveling with younger children. A better option is to come between March and May when

▲ *Banff National Park, Alberta, Canada*
© KAREN SCHALER

you can still enjoy all the winter activities without turning into a Popsicle every time you go outside.

Part of picking a smart, family-friendly destination is choosing a place where you actually spend time with your family, doing things together. A novel idea, I know, but if you're truly trying to reconnect with your children, it's not going to do much good if the kids take off in one direction and you take off in another and all of you just meet up for dinner. The whole idea behind this Travel Therapy vacation is to actually find activities you can all do together as a family—and Banff and Lake Louise have a long list of options.

One of my favorite ways to spend the morning and see the scenery is a dog sledding trip through the Rockies. Dog sledding has been around for thousands of years, and there are several different tour operators in the Banff/Lake Louise area to choose from. I like Kingmik Dog Sled Tours, open since 1982, because their tour operator is the only one allowed to operate inside the protected Banff National Park.

Each sled holds two people, and before starting, you're bundled up in a cocoon of blankets to keep you warm. If you want to take pictures, you'd better have your camera ready, because once the dogs take off running, it's hard to move around in the sled. One of the highlights that all kids—and even adults—seem to love is when the musher

stops and gives them a chance to stand on the back of the sled to lead the team. Of course, the musher stays with the kids to make sure they don't fall off. I've seen children as young as three give it a try. They love it so much that the only downside is their not wanting to get back into the sled.

Spring is also an excellent time to do some skiing. And for family members ready for a challenge, there's a really cool new activity called snowbiking. For this adventure, you basically get on a bike that has skis instead of tires and your feet get strapped into two mini-skis. It's not as hard as it looks, and kids especially love the thrill of shredding down a snowy slope. If you're looking for a tamer option, ice-hiking is also popular in this area. For these treks you hook special ice cleats to your boots and navigate slippery ice paths through steep canyons and across frozen lakes. It's easy to take a guided tour, or you can venture out on your own. One of the most popular ice-hiking choices is Johnston Canyon, outside of Banff, where you can spend about an hour and a half making your way up to the canyon's famed upper falls. While this trek is free to the public, it's a smart choice to sign up with a tour operator like Discover Banff Tours (www.banfftours .com). The guides pick you up at your hotel, drive you to the canyon, and provide the ice cleats and tips you'll need for navigating the steel catwalk that is suspended from the canyon walls.

There's also the long-standing favorites of cross-country skiing and snowshoeing, and you can even find a beautiful outdoor ice skating rink at the Fairmont Chateau Lake Louise, a grand hotel that looks like a fairytale castle nestled right next to a lake. Even if you don't stay at the hotel, stop by for some hot chocolate because the views from this property are phenomenal. For more on the best places to stay and how to explore this unique and inspiring TRAVEL THERAPY destination, you can find out all you need to know at the official website for Banff Lake Louise Tourism, www.banfflakelouise.com, which has some fantastic video clips.

 DESTINATION: *Paradise Island, Caribbean*

A tropical beach vacation may be just what you need to de-stress and have some fun together as a family, and one of the top family-friendly destinations in the Caribbean is Paradise Island (www.nassauparadiseisland .com) in the Bahamas. Any time you mention Paradise Island to people who have been there, they will usually ask if you went to Atlantis. This family-oriented, award-winning resort is actually a destination in itself, with close to four thousand guest rooms ranging in price from moderate to top dollar.

What makes Atlantis so popular is how the entire resort caters to families who want a quality vacation experience. Atlantis has eleven sensational swimming pools with some of the most impressive waterslides in the world. These slides are so cool that even adults get in on the action. One standout slide is a six-story Mayan temple where there are five different daring options. If you're feeling gutsy, go for the Leap of Faith slide. You plunge sixty feet in an almost complete vertical drop and then shoot through a clear tunnel that's actually submerged in a lagoon of real sharks.

Atlantis also has three impressive aquariums with more than fifty thousand fish, sharks, and manta rays, and its own water park. There's also a beautiful beach with every water sport imaginable and twenty-one restaurants on the site. That's why people say Atlantis isn't just a resort—it's an actual destination!

On the Atlantis website (www.atlantis .com), you'll find a long list of activities the entire family can enjoy, including the lazy river ride where you float on inner tubes down a river that's located on the property; the Atlantis Theatre, where you can nibble on popcorn and watch recently released movies; and a library with more than twelve hundred books in stock. They even take care of the smallest guests with a Gentle Travel Kit that includes baby bath soap and lotions. If you've spent enough time bonding and need a break, there are a number of different programs for tweens and teens at the Atlantis Kids Club. If you're looking to go out in the evening and your kids are pooped out, there's even a babysitting service where the sitter comes to your room.

If you can pry yourself—and more important, your children—away from Atlantis, there are some other interesting options for families on Paradise Island. Top choices include interacting with dolphins at the Dolphin Encounter on Blue Lagoon Island and visiting the Ardastra Gardens, Zoo & Conservation Center, the only zoo in the Bahamas.

ROUGHING IT TOGETHER
Camping Adventures

Whether you're looking to reconnect with your children, a family member, or even a love interest, one way to focus on a relationship is to escape all the usual distractions by traveling off the beaten path—literally.

When I was young and living in the Northwest, I spent a lot of my weekends camping because it was the easy and cheap thing to do. My mom loves fishing, so our trips usually involved hiking, fishing, and then setting up camp for the night. Those trips stand out as some of the best times my mom and I spent together. We didn't have a fancy setup with a television or radio. It was before iPods and BlackBerrys, so we would be out in the middle of nowhere with only each other to talk to. Sure, as I got older and entered my teen years, I would grumble about having

to go camping all the time, and by the time I moved to California before my senior year of high school, I was more than ready to leave my hiking boots and fishing pole behind.

As the years rushed by, camping was never on my vacation "to do" list. My mom continued to go, but my schedule was too hectic and the timing never seemed right. I obviously needed some TRAVEL THERAPY back then but just didn't know it. Then it seemed like in a blink of an eye, my mom had outgrown the ruggedness of sleeping in a tent, so we didn't have the chance to camp together again. That's when I realized those camping trips, and more importantly our time spent together fishing and hiking, were priceless.

Camping, if you do it right and leave all the electronic gadgets at home, is an excellent TRAVEL THERAPY for spending quality time with someone. On a camping adventure, you're all working toward the same goal, whether it's hiking up a mountain, pitching a tent, or trying to catch your next dinner. Instead of watching videos, you can play cards or share stories. I have found that it's often the quiet moments with someone you remember most.

SMILE! *PHOTOGRAPHY TIPS*

When you're camping in the wild, chances are you'll run into some fascinating wildlife that you'll want to take pictures of. Every year people around the world are killed because they get too close to an animal when they're trying to get the perfect shot. Here are some simple tips to help you get the best shots without putting yourself in danger.

- Never approach a wild animal.
- Photograph wildlife from the safety of your vehicle.
- Make sure you have a way out in case the animal charges.
- Use telephoto lenses.
- Make sure the sun is behind you when shooting.
- Observe animals quietly.
- Never feed wild animals.

DESTINATION: *Washington State*

I've always said Washington State is one of the most beautiful places to camp if you can find a day when it's not raining! That aside, there are some spectacular camping opportunities throughout the Pacific Northwest, including in my favorite area—the Cascade Mountains.

The Cascades run all the way from California to British Columbia. The stretch that goes through Washington is filled with hundreds of miles of hiking trails, pristine lakes, fish-filled streams, and some of the most stunning mountain scenery you'll ever find.

▲ *Camping in Washington State*
© WASHINGTON STATE TOURISM

The smartest way to get the lay of the land is to go to the Washington State Tourism website (www.experiencewa.com), where you can find answers to questions you haven't even thought to ask. Besides the usual long list of places to stay and must-see tourist attractions, there is also a special link dedicated just to camping. Click on the link and you'll get the inside scoop on all the major campgrounds throughout the state; there are literally dozens to choose from. The tourism folks tell me they update the site often, so you'll be able to get current information on all the different camping opportunities, including what's available and how to reserve a site.

For many of the most popular spots, you'll want to reserve your site early, especially if you're looking for a campground during the popular summer months. Still, no matter what time of year you want to take your trip, you should be able to find something available because there are so many different camping areas to choose from.

Since the Washington State Tourism website's camping list can be a little overwhelming, it's a good idea to narrow down your choice by selecting an area of the Cascades you want to explore. The Cascades in the southern part of the state include the famed Mount Rainier. It's the tallest mountain peak in the state, towering almost 14,500 feet high. People come from all over the world to make this challenging climb. The southern part of the Cascades is also where you'll find Mount St. Helens. This mountain was made famous in 1980 when a huge volcanic eruption killed several dozen people and destroyed more than two hundred homes. It still spouts small amounts of ash occasionally, but it's nothing that threatens touring the area.

At the other end of the range are the North Cascades. This is where I grew up camping—around the Ross Lake National Recreation Area, Lake Wenatchee, and Lake Chelan. Here you'll find Mount Baker, a great ski resort in the winter, and the North Cascades National Park. If you're starting your trip from the Seattle area and don't have a lot of time, another great option is hitting the Central Cascades, where you have all kinds of different camping options just a few hours from Seattle's center.

No matter where you decide to go or what time of year you're planning to travel, it's always a good idea to bring some rain gear along. According to a local weatherman at KOMO-TV, Seattle averages 155 days of rain a year. But look on the bright side—it's one of the reasons why Washington is so green and gorgeous.

"It was during many, many wild and random road trips with a small group of friends, where we all helped each other to feel free but still connected to each other, that we lived by a quote from Henry David Thoreau that started with:

'I went to the woods because I wanted to live deliberately; I wanted to live deep and suck out all the marrow of life . . . '"

—HOPE QUITORIANO, RETAIL MANAGER, ARIZONA

DESTINATION: *Grand Canyon National Park, Nevada/Arizona*

"Wow!" was the first thing I said when I saw the Grand Canyon up close and personal. I know it sounds cliché, but even after seeing hundreds of photos of the Grand Canyon, nothing prepared me for the actual experience of standing on the rim and taking in the scenery of this surreal place. Its size alone is overwhelming. The National Park Service website gives the Grand Canyon's dimensions as 277 miles long, up to eighteen miles wide, and one mile deep (www.nps.gov/grca).

Unbelievable! When you're standing above this massive canyon, it's easy to imagine how you could spend the rest of your life trying to explore this marvel and yet never even scratch the surface.

That's why the Grand Canyon offers the ultimate TRAVEL THERAPY camping adventure. But first you need to decide how rugged you want to get. The National Park Service says most people visit the Canyon's South Rim because it's open year-round and is located in Arizona. The North Rim is more out of the way and harder to navigate; it's much more secluded, but that could be just the ticket if you're looking for a true camping escape.

Before you venture out, you'll want to check the National Park Service website for the latest conditions and camping rules and regulations. The North Rim has a shorter season as this section of the park is only open from May through October, so if you're planning to pitch your tent here, book your site well in advance.

Camping in the Grand Canyon gives you the rare opportunity to inhale inspiration and exhale stress. Every time I visit, I'm amazed by the canyon's sheer size and magnificence. Camping is one of the best ways to feel connected to this ancient land, allowing you to wake up with the sunrise and follow the rhythm of a day. Camping in the Grand Canyon is a rare treat, and one experience you'll never forget.

If you're searching for more information about the Grand Canyon, another recommended site is www.grandcanyonvisitor bureau.com, run by the Grand Canyon Chamber & Visitor's Bureau. Here you'll find not only updated information about the best camp sites, but also some good updates about restaurants and hotels in the area in case you want to trade in your tent for a comfy bed.

▶ *Hiking Trail in the Grand Canyon*
© NATIONAL PARK SERVICE

DESTINATION: *Yellowstone National Park, Idaho/Montana/Wyoming*

Heading to Yellowstone National Park for your family camping outing allows you to be a part of history—a cool option for many families. When Yellowstone opened in 1872, it was America's first national park; and over the decades Yellowstone has continued to impress. Many people get confused about exactly where Yellowstone is because the park sprawls across all three states of Idaho, Montana, and Wyoming, and it's known for its sensational scenery and wildlife sighting opportunities.

You're always warned when camping inside Yellowstone not to leave any food out because it attracts animals, especially bears. I remember as a child always trying to leave something out because, of course, I was a kid and I wanted to see a bear—or any animal for that matter. Not smart, I quickly learned, because if an animal comes into the camp you often have to leave, and there goes your vacation!

If you are staying in Yellowstone, there are strict rules about what to do when you spot an animal, and they don't include going right up to the animal and taking its picture. Park regulations say that you have to stay at least twenty-five yards away from a bison and one hundred yards away from any bear. For photography tips, check out the sidebar on page 105.

For an updated list of the best camping areas inside Yellowstone, you can go to the National Park Service website at www.nps .gov. This site has the rundown on all the different campsites, including if the amenities include flushing toilets and showers. Most of the campsites are above six thousand feet, so even in the summer it gets chilly at night and you'll want to plan accordingly. Another good thing to know is that seven of the campsites in Yellowstone are first come first serve, and they're usually filled by eleven in the morning, so if you have your eye on one of these spots you'd better stake it out early. The National Park Service says you're only allowed to camp for fourteen days, so as beautiful as it is, don't get too addicted to your spot. Also, be sure to have a good map with you when you're traveling around the park. It's easy to get turned around, and while part of the adventure is exploring new places, it's not so fun when you're completely lost, tired, and hungry.

Summer is obviously the peak tourist time in the park, and people come from all over the world by the thousands. If your goal is trying to spot some wildlife, know that your chances will improve greatly if you visit the park in the spring or early fall when the crowds aren't as heavy. If you find yourself in the park with the crowds though, consider getting up early to see the best wildlife.

ONE AND ONLY
Escape For Couples

If you've reached a point in your relationship where you're not even sure why you're in the relationship in the first place, then you are more than overdue for some serious TRAVEL THERAPY. Right now you can't afford to mess around; your future with your loved one is on the line. Chances are if you're having doubts, so is your partner. If you believe you might still be able to salvage your relationship if you could just talk and spend some time together, then what are you waiting for? Pack your bags and journey to one of the following TRAVEL THERAPY destinations, where the emphasis is on couples-only activities.

By putting yourself and your significant other in a situation where you can relax and focus on each other, the hope is you'll find your way back to that place where you can't imagine life without the other person. Experiencing new people, places, and things together can often create a new bond that's unbreakable.

DESTINATION: *Principality Of Monaco*

Champagne? *Oui!* Ah, there's nothing like a toast with a glass of fabulous champagne to kick off a vacation, right? The glamorous and glitzy Monaco is the perfect TRAVEL THERAPY pick if you're craving an escape of the adult variety. This fascinating little country, about the size of New York City's Central Park, defines chic, yet there is an underlying charm here that keeps it real.

Before you can truly appreciate what Monaco has to offer, you have to understand a bit about this nation's unique history. Monaco is a principality located on the Mediterranean Sea. It's the second smallest country in the world behind Vatican City. The Grimaldi family has reigned over Monaco for more than seven hundred years, and Prince Rainier III, who made worldwide headlines in 1956 when he married American actress Grace Kelly, ruled the country from 1949 until his death in 2005. Prince Rainier III and Princess Grace's son, H.S.H. Prince Albert, currently serves as the country's head of state. For more about Monaco's fascinating background, your best resource is the consulate's website at www.monaco-consulate.com.

The most well-known area in Monaco is Monte Carlo, the perfect adult playground, with its world-class casinos and clubs and fantastic hotels and restaurants. Monte Carlo is also where you'll find some of Monaco's best hotels and restaurants. There are several different tour options that give you an overview of Monaco, but probably the most stunning view is from a helicopter. Also, because Monaco is so small, a fun way to get around once you have your bearings is to rent a scooter.

If you want to do more than lie on the beach, you won't have any problem staying busy because this small speck of paradise has a lot to offer. You can hit the links for some golf at the Monte Carlo Country Club or try some deep-sea diving, sailing, or fishing.

Just make sure the activities you choose are something you can do together, because the whole idea behind this trip is finding ways to reconnect.

After the sun goes down, Monaco heats up with a dazzling nightlife, so be sure to bring your best party attire. This is one place where you can't have enough bling! For more on the different places you can stay when visiting Monaco, and for a list of special events like the famed Formula One Grand Prix, check out the official website of the Monaco Government Tourist Office and Convention Authority at www.visitmonaco.com.

▲ *Port Hercules, Monaco's Harbor*
© MONACO GOVERNMENT TOURIST OFFICE

"After a rough year for our relationship, my husband and I were searching for a place to celebrate our ten-year anniversary and chose the California wine country where we'd spent our honeymoon. The country is so beautiful and peaceful, and we found great people, wonderful spas, amazing restaurants, and of course, the WINE! I literally felt my pulse slow the moment we arrived, and my husband and I were able to reconnect and remember all the things we love so much about each other."

—Kristin Kelly, VP of Communications, Texas

Destination: Sonoma County, California

The first time I visited this Travel Therapy destination, I was completely enchanted by how quaint and charming the area is. I had been to Napa Valley and fought the crowds during the wine-tasting rush, which was why I was surprised to find Sonoma so laid-back and relaxing. The fact that this stretch of California wine country also has more than two hundred wineries (including some of my favorites, like Simi, Château St. Jean, and Ferrari-Carano) makes it the perfect place to settle in for a few days of pampering your palate by tasting some award-winning wines and cuisine. You can also pamper your body by checking into one of the area's forty different spas, many of which have romantic massage options for couples. What makes a spa visit unique in Sonoma County is how the different properties specialize in using local ingredients like grape seeds, honey, and even goat's milk.

Before you get to Sonoma, do some research to select a few top wineries you'd like to visit, and set up your appointments ahead of time. At some wineries in Sonoma Valley you can just drop by for a tasting, but an increasing number are now asking that you have an appointment on the books.

To research where you want to go and to make sure you have the reservations you need, check out the Sonoma County Tourism Bureau (www.sonomacounty.com). This website has an extensive listing of Sonoma wineries, including information about how each operation is run, whether or not you need to make an appointment for a tasting, and if there's a charge. I know a lot of first-time visitors are disappointed when they stop by their favorite winery only to be told they can't do a tasting because they didn't make an appointment, so be sure you plan ahead so you don't miss out.

The bureau's website also gives you an extensive list of hotels, restaurants, spas, and other things to do in the area in case you want to take a quick break from your wine tasting.

Another great benefit about visiting wine country in Sonoma County is the location—it's only about a half hour away from San Francisco. You can even pick a hotel in the Bay Area, and then arrange to have a driver take you to the wine tasting. This is a great idea especially if you plan to do a lot of tastings so you don't have to drink and drive. If you pick this option, start early in the morning because the roads from San Francisco up to the wine region can get crowded. I personally enjoy staying right in the heart of Sonoma County and experiencing all that wine country has to offer and saving San Francisco for another trip.

▲ *Merlot Grapes Ready for Harvest at Ravenswood Winery*
© PETER GRIFFIN/SONOMA COUNTY TOURISM BUREAU

DESTINATION: *Matamanoa Island, Fiji*

It's true you always remember your first love, and I fell in love with Matamanoa Island back in the late 1980s when I was wrapping up a month-long trip to Australia, New Zealand, and Fiji. I was traveling with my step-mom, who had surprised me with the trip, and the grand finale was staying at Matamanoa Island, in Fiji's Mamanuca Islands.

This was my first experience staying on a private island, so Matamanoa will always have a special place in my heart. I knew from the moment my toes touched the sand that my travel dreams would never be the same. Once you get a taste of a private island experience, it's hard to go back to crowded tourist traps.

What makes Matamanoa Island so special is how isolated and remote it is, and how you feel like you practically have the entire island to yourself. There are only twenty beachfront *bures* (villas) and thirteen garden-view hotel rooms on the entire island.

The atmosphere is low-key, and to keep things quiet and simple the resort doesn't allow children under twelve years old. The focus of Matamanoa is on adults who are looking to get away from it all, and that means no screeching children. You also won't find any television sets or Internet connections in the rooms. This is the kind of destination where you can truly let go of all that's bothering you and concentrate on being together as a couple and enjoying each other's company. There's even a small spa that offers a few simple services like massages, manicures, and pedicures.

After a few days of soaking up the sun, if you're looking to get out on the turquoise blue water, there are several different glass-bottom boat trips you can take where you can do some snorkeling or choose to never leave the boat but still do some fantastic coral viewing. If you're feeling more adventurous, you can sign up for a mountain hike or play some beach cricket or—one of my favorites—go coconut bowling. If you want to just sit back with a cool drink and be entertained, check out the coconut husking and cracking demonstration or learn how to speak Fijian. You can find a list of cultural activities on Matamanoa's website at www.matamanoa.com.

Matamanoa's magic is in the transformation you feel after just a few hours on the island. The merry-go-round of life slows down enough for you to catch your breath, clear your cluttered mind, and reprioritize what you want to do in life—and whom you want to do it with. You leave the island feeling refreshed and rejuvenated, like you can handle anything and anyone, and the magic that is Matamanoa stays with you for a lifetime.

> "Going to Hawaii wasn't on my 'bucket' list but riding a surfboard was, so at sixty-four years old I set out to fulfill a lifelong dream. What an amazing feeling to find out that I wasn't too old to ride the waves. Who knows what I'll do next. . . . "

> —LAO SCHALER, RETIRED SCHOOL TEACHER, WASHINGTON

AUTHOR'S PICK

 DESTINATION: *Hawaii*

There was no way my tiny five-foot-four mother was going to outdo me by learning to surf while I sat on the beach like a baby because I was too afraid I would crash and burn. My athletic mother has always loved swimming. I, on the other hand, have never felt very comfortable in the water. When I lived in California, I watched too many surfers wipe out and get tossed by the waves or smacked around by their boards. It didn't look like fun to me—not even a little bit.

But then, on one of our mother/daughter trips, standing on Waikiki Beach in Hawaii, my mom told me that surfing was something she had always wanted to try. To make matters worse, the hotel we were staying at, the Halekulani, offered free private surf lessons as part of our stay in the luxurious Vera Wang Suite. When my mom heard the news about the free lessons, she looked like a kid

at Christmas; and so, gritting my teeth and plastering a smile on my face, I agreed that, "Yes, learning to surf could be fun."

Our instructor, Ty, was also adorable, so now there were two reasons I couldn't wimp out. I didn't even flinch when he pointed at a monstrous long board that was three times as tall as I was and told me that would be my ride. My petite mom got the smaller, more normal-looking board. Ty only spent about five minutes with us on the beach, giving us a quick lesson on how to stand up on a surfboard, before getting us right in the water. Looking back, this was probably a good thing because I didn't have time to ask too many questions or really think about what I was doing. He helped us paddle out a safe distance

▶ *Surfing Hawaii Style*
© HAWAII TOURISM AUTHORITY/STEWART PINSKY

from the beach and then explained what we needed to do. He would hold on to the back of our boards, and when he told us to start paddling we would need to paddle our hearts out until he told us to stand up.

The waves started to pick up, thrilling both Ty and my mom, and I just kept a grin plastered on my face wondering what in the heck I had gotten myself into. My gutsy mom volunteered to go first. My heart raced when I watched the waves come crashing in and my mom start paddling. When Ty yelled, "Stand up!" she only hesitated for a moment before doing the move we'd been shown on the beach. I held my breath as she wobbled just a little bit, but then stayed up and rode her first wave about one hundred feet before losing her balance and tipping over. I'll never forget the smile on her face and how her eyes gleamed with victory when she popped out of the water. She looked as if she'd just won an Olympic gold medal.

When it was my turn, my normally quiet mom was quite the cheerleader. The waves seemed to be getting even bigger, making me even more nervous. While we waited for the "perfect" wave, I asked Ty all kinds of questions: How far forward should I go on the board? Where should my weight be? How do I fall? But instead of answering me, he kept his eyes on the waves and then started yelling, "Paddle, paddle, paddle!" I wasn't ready, but the waves didn't wait, and it was only a second before I heard him yelling, "Stand up!"

I must have hesitated, because then came a series of yells: "Stand up, stand up, stand up!" The memory of my mom's successful attempt flashed in my mind and I jumped up on the board just as I felt this surge of power from the wave propelling me forward. Flying across my first wave was an amazing adrenaline rush. I was surfing! A few seconds later, I lost my balance and went tumbling into the water. I was attached to my board by a leash around my ankle, so when I went one way and my board flew the other, I felt like Gumby being pulled in two different directions. Thankfully, seconds later when it was over I found the surface and came sputtering up for air.

I could hear my mom and Ty hooting and hollering. I had done it. We had both done it. My mom and I had learned something together, and we'd shared this extraordinary experience. We stayed out surfing for another hour before going back to our room exhausted but exhilarated. It turns out I love surfing, and sharing this discovery with my mom made it even more special. My mother and I are different in so many ways, but on that day—the day we learned to surf—we were linked by a common experience that we'll both cherish forever.

After the good luck we had with our first surfing lesson, we recommend getting a private lesson your first time out, whether that is solo or with a group. A private lesson is much more personal, and a good instructor like Ty will tailor the way he teaches to fit your personality. Plus, if you have two people you can split the cost.

With more than thirty years of experience, Ty started surfing as soon as he could walk. He has his own school, specializing in private lessons that are quite affordable. You can usually find him on the beach around the Halekulani Resort. For more on his surfing school you can go to his website at www .tygurneysurfschool.com.

If you're interested in checking out some other surf schools on Oahu, go to the Oahu Visitors Bureau website at www.visit -oahu.com. There you'll find a long list of surfing options, including a program called Girls Who Surf that features all female surf instructors.

"As a busy professional and mother of three, I've enjoyed traveling with my family as a way to reconnect and spend valuable time with people who are most important in my life. Traveling together we form new bonds as we uncover not only amazing treasures around the world, but also unique facets of one another."

—RACHEL SACCO, PRESIDENT AND CEO OF
SCOTTSDALE CONVENTION AND VISITORS BUREAU, ARIZONA

Reconnecting Vacation Checklist

CHOOSE TRIPS WHERE YOU CAN:

- Spend time with each other
- Enjoy the same activities
- Don't have work distractions
- Can relax and rejuvenate
- Can escape daily stresses
- Can reconnect and bond

"The world is a book, and those who do not travel read only one page."

—SAINT AUGUSTINE

Chapter 6

Doctor's Orders

*B*ouncing back after a surgery or difficult illness can challenge you to your very core. Weeks after the doctor gives you the thumbs-up and says you've "recovered," you find yourself still feeling listless and struggling to fight off the blues. If battling your illness zapped all your energy and enthusiasm, you need a healthy dose of TRAVEL THERAPY to help get your mental and physical strength back. The great news is that as soon as you're ready to travel, there are some terrific TRAVEL THERAPY destinations that are just what the doctor ordered to help you reenergize your body, mind, and spirit!

It's your choice whether you fall into that toxic pattern of feeling weak and sick all the time, or whether you can stand up and prove to the world and yourself that you're ready to get back out there and join the land of the living again.

Here are three TRAVEL THERAPY ideas to help you move forward, one step at a time:

- Beach Bumming—Best Beaches
- Pamper Your Spirit—Spa Vacations
- Home Away from Home—Vacation Home Rentals

If you're having a hard time deciding between these three options, just take this simple and painless TRAVEL THERAPY quiz to point you in the right direction.

◀ *Four Seasons Resort, Maui at Wailea, Hawaii*
© FOUR SEASONS RESORT MAUI

TRAVEL THERAPY QUIZ

1 You're in the mood for:

  a. Wiggling your toes in the sand

  b. A relaxing massage or facial

  c. Reading a book at home

2 You'd rather:

  a. Lounge on a beach

  b. Chill at a spa

  c. Kick back on the couch

3 You're ready for:

  a. Sun and surf

  b. A fluffy robe and slippers

  c. A homemade meal

4 You'd rather stay:

  a. At the beach

  b. At a spa

  c. At a home

5 The idea of renting someone's beach home:

  a. Might be okay

  b. Doesn't sound fun

  c. Sounds perfect

6 A great meal would be:

  a. Surf and turf

  b. Something healthy

  c. A barbeque

7 You're willing to travel:

  a. An unlimited amount

  b. Only as far as you need to

  c. Not out of the country

8 Right now you need:

  a. A walk on the beach

  b. A good spa treatment

  c. A "home away from home"

9 You would rather:

  a. Get outside

  b. Be pampered

  c. Change your environment

TRAVEL THERAPY DIAGNOSIS

If you're looking at your answers and most are "A," then you'll want to grab your beach bag and sunglasses and check out the TRAVEL THERAPY options under Beach Bumming. If it turns out that most of your picks are under the "B" category, then it's time to Pamper Your Spirit at one of the top TRAVEL THERAPY spa destinations in the United States. Finally, if "C" is your answer of choice, then what you need is a Home Away from Home—and TRAVEL THERAPY has you covered. If it ends up that you have answers in all three categories, then lucky you—you can pick from any of the TRAVEL THERAPY choices you find in this chapter.

DESTINATIONS TO AVOID:

- Anywhere too stressful
- Anyplace loud and annoying
- Destinations where you don't like the food
- Destinations where the weather's cold and damp
- Places where you can't relax
- Places where the pace is hectic

"*There is good reason the fourteenth chapter of Leviticus in the Bible encouraged us to travel; it helps us make positive changes and start fresh, lower stress, become more creative, and live longer.*"

—DR. JOHN D. LENTZ, MARRIAGE & FAMILY THERAPIST
AND ORDAINED MINISTER, INDIANA

BEACH BUMMING
Best Beaches

I always head to the beach whenever my energy reserve hits rock bottom and I need a quick pick-me-up. Just the simple gesture of taking off my shoes and wiggling my toes in the sand seems to help chase any troubled thoughts away. The moment I arrive at this TRAVEL THERAPY destination, it's as if someone flips a switch and I'm able to breathe a little deeper and finally relax. There's just something so mesmerizing about watching the waves crash against the shore. The beach never lets me down. Its energy is healing—mentally and physically.

Depending on where you are in your recovery, you may just want to find a chair or towel and plop down on the beach. You can spend your day doing nothing more than relaxing, catching up on your sleep, or getting lost in your favorite book. If you can't find a shady spot, be sure to protect yourself against the sun with a large hat and a generous slathering of sunscreen. The last thing you need is to wake up burned to a crisp.

If the beach brings out your energetic side, you're in luck. The following three TRAVEL THERAPY destinations have dozens of cool options to help you lay low while still being entertained. The goal of a sun, surf, and sand vacation is to let go of your daily stress and worries and surrender to the beach bumming way of life, where the biggest decision you should have to make is which bathing suit to wear.

"Turks and Caicos was the perfect destination for seclusion, relaxation, and pampering. With the pristine beaches, amazing sunsets, and the exotic island fare, Grace Bay Beach was the perfect getaway."

—KELLY HERKERT, SALES EXECUTIVE, NEW JERSEY

 DESTINATION: *Grace Bay Beach, Turks And Caicos*

With sand as soft as baby powder and water that gives new meaning to the color blue, Grace Bay Beach on Turks and Caicos is one of those breathtaking destinations where your stress melts away almost immediately. I first heard about Grace Bay Beach in the early 1980s when Club Med (www.clubmed.us) opened up the first large resort in the area. Once people started discovering Grace Bay Beach, it began winning numerous awards and accolades. It is even labeled by some as one of the most beautiful beaches in the world. In the early 1990s, other luxury resorts like Grace Bay Club (www.gracebayclub.com) caught on and more hotels started sprouting up along this sexy strip of beach in the British West Indies. Turks and Caicos quickly

▲ *Grace Bay Beach, Provo, Turks and Caicos*
© KAREN SCHALER

changed from a quaint little island chain that didn't even have electricity to a hot spot on the top-rated tourism circuit. Now there are more than three-dozen world-class beachfront properties along Grace Bay Beach, but the beach, which is twelve miles long, still has a secluded, peaceful feeling. Grace Bay Beach is on the island of Providenciales, nicknamed Provo. Provo is the most popular of the forty islands that make up the Turks and Caicos archipelago, which is located less than six hundred miles from Miami.

The first thing you'll notice when you get to the beach, besides the picture-perfect scenery, is how incredibly soft the sand is. On my first trip to Grace Bay Beach I was so surprised and fascinated I literally stopped and leaned down to pick up the sand and rub some of the powdery substance between my fingers. It is white as snow, and it doesn't have that granular texture of most sands; instead it feels soft and silky. The brochures aren't lying.

You'll find one of the most beautiful sections of Grace Bay Beach in front of the Regent Palms (www.regenthotels.com/thepalms), an upscale property with an award-winning spa and restaurant and 164 luxury rooms and suites. Here the beach is wide and not very crowded, making it the ideal spot if you're looking for a quiet escape. The resort doesn't allow motorized water sports in front of the property, so the atmosphere is soothing and peaceful. If you're staying at the resort there

are plenty of other water activities, like sailing and kayaking, which are offered to guests for free, and you'll get spoiled by the beach butlers who come by and spritz you down with cool water and deliver delicious complimentary treats.

Grace Bay Beach is open to the public, so even if you're staying nearby, take a walk and see what it has to offer. Keep in mind the beach chairs and special amenities are for resort guests only.

When you're picking a beachfront property, it's a good idea to do your homework ahead of time so you can find the atmosphere you're looking for. A great place to start is the official Turks and Caicos Tourist Board website (www.turksandcaicostourism.com), which has constantly updated information about the resorts, restaurants, spas, and beaches.

Part of the draw to Turks and Caicos is how easy it is to get to with direct flights from various locations like New York City, Miami, Charlotte, Boston, Atlanta, Toronto, and London. The direct flight from New York City takes approximately three and half hours.

Of Turks and Caicos's forty islands, only a handful are developed. But if you find you love Grace Bay Beach, you might want to do a little island hopping and check out some of the other more undiscovered options like North Caicos, Middle Caicos, Grand Turk, and the ultra-exclusive private island of Parrot Cay.

DESTINATION: *Santa Monica Beach, Santa Monica, California*

What I love about Santa Monica Beach is that it's easy to get to and it's affordable. Okay, sure, some might argue that nothing in Southern California is affordable, but if you compare Santa Monica Beach with some other top beach communities in the Caribbean, Europe, Mexico, and Hawaii, and you factor in your savings by opting to stay closer to home, you can actually save money by heading to Santa Monica.

Of course, if you're looking to splurge, Santa Monica has more than its share of fabulous hotel properties. Some of my favorites include the Viceroy Santa Monica, the Fairmont Miramar Hotel & Bungalows, Shutters on the Beach, and Le Merigot. But in Santa Monica, you can also find more modest options, all the way down to budget. The best way to scope out the area is to head to the Santa Monica Convention and Visitors Bureau's website at www.santamonica.com. This website lists not only a plethora of hotel options, but also gives you the inside track on some of the best restaurants in the area. It also includes a long list of other things to do in Santa Monica if you want to venture away from the beach. At this Travel Therapy destination, you'll quickly find you can go as big or as little as your pocketbook allows.

Santa Monica Beach is also a smart choice if you do not want to leave the States, but you still want that feeling of a first-class beach vacation. Santa Monica Beach is bordered by Malibu Beach and Venice Beach, and it's just eight miles from Los Angeles International Airport. There are actually two "official" beaches in Santa Monica: Santa Monica State Beach and Will Rogers State Beach. Both are fantastic for swimming, surfing, and playing volleyball.

This Southern California beach is also an excellent place to rent a bike, rollerblades, or even old-fashioned roller skates. There's a paved path that runs the stretch of the beach and rental fees are reasonable. Some of my best memories are of biking, running, or skating along this path. If you're visiting during the popular summer months, your best option is to try the path early in the morning before it gets too crowded, or just before sunset.

A trip to Santa Monica wouldn't be complete without a stop at the Santa Monica Pier, the oldest pier on the West Coast. Opened in 1909, the pier now has all sorts of fun things to check out, including an aquarium, a working wooden horse carousel (open since 1922), and the world's first solar-powered Ferris wheel. There are also a handful of restaurants and a fresh fish market.

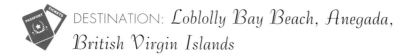

DESTINATION: *Loblolly Bay Beach, Anegada, British Virgin Islands*

If you're feeling strong enough to travel to the British Virgin Islands, then there's one beach you shouldn't miss: Loblolly Bay Beach. This is a beach that's absolutely worth the time it takes to travel there.

If you're asking, "Lob what? Where is that?" that's perfect! This is exactly why this beach is so special—because most people have never even heard of it. I've visited this ultra-secluded beach several times over the last fifteen years and always worry it's going to become "discovered." I have nightmares about visiting and finding the beach lined with hotels and packed with people. Thankfully, the beach has hardly changed over the past decade. It's considered crowded if you see more than a dozen people.

That said, some people may wonder why I would share this best-kept secret, one of my personal favorite escapes. Here's why: It's hard on your body, mind, and spirit to get over a serious illness, and if sharing this TRAVEL THERAPY destination helps even one person, I'm all for it. After all, that's what this book is all about, sharing the best of the best.

I discovered Loblolly Bay Beach on my first sailing trip in the British Virgin Islands in the 1990s. I had heard about an island called Anegada, where most charter sailors aren't allowed to go to because of a treacherous reef surrounding the island that's said to have caused more than two hundred shipwrecks. Of course, this made me want to go more. I'm always searching out those places that most people don't go to in hopes of finding a secret paradise. I made sure the captain on the sailboat I chartered was qualified to sail to Anegada. He warned us that we might not be able to get close enough to go ashore if the weather conditions didn't cooperate. Still, we decided to give it a shot.

We were in luck! We were able to anchor off the island and take our dinghy to the dock. Once we got ashore, we asked the only two people on the dock where the best beach was. They told us it was on the other side of the island and we would have to take a cab. "A cab?" I asked, mystified because there were no cars in sight, only a dirt road. I was skeptical, but within ten minutes a pickup truck showed up with some makeshift seats in the flatbed. After a bumpy ride we were deposited in front of a narrow path, and our driver told us to just walk through the thick tropical foliage and we'd find the beach—and we found one of the most spectacular beaches I've ever seen.

I was speechless. There wasn't another soul on the beach, and I felt like the world had opened up and dropped me onto one of the most magnificent stretches of beach.

At Loblolly Bay Beach, the turquoise water is crystal clear; in some areas the water is so shallow you can walk fifty feet out into the ocean. The snorkeling is phenomenal. Within the first few minutes, I was swimming with sea turtles and dozens of angelfish, parrot fish, and triggerfish. For the more daring snorkelers and divers, there are also a number of caves and tunnels to explore just off the main part of the beach. I could have spent the entire day in the water, but it was good to discover that there are two tiny places to eat along the beach: Big Bamboo and Flash of Beauty. Both offer simple fare, the favorite being the conch fritters and lobster that's caught right off the beach.

▲ *Loblolly Beach, Anegada Island in the British Virgin Islands*
© KAREN SCHALER

To appreciate how rare a beach like Loblolly is you need a better understanding of Anegada, which is only about ten miles long and two miles wide, and is the only coral island in the British Virgin Islands. Anegada, meaning "drowned island," got its name because the island's highest point is only twenty-eight feet above sea level. On Anegada, you'll find everything from beautiful birds, like blue herons and sandpipers, to impressive foliage, like sea lavender and exotic orchids.

Anegada is like a place that time forgot, but things are changing. You can now find several taxi options on the island and you can even rent a car, although I never saw one.

Anegada's beauty is rugged and untamed, but places to stay are starting to sprout up along the beach, so things won't always stay so secluded. It used to be that the only way to reach the island was by sailboat, but now you can fly there in a small plane from Tortola, or you can charter a plane from Virgin Gorda or Saint Thomas.

If this sounds like a great TRAVEL THERAPY option, I would recommend going sooner than later so you, too, can experience the magic of this unspoiled island and have your own priceless moment of seeing something so beautiful you're left speechless. For more about what you can find on Anegada, log on to www.bvitourism.com.

TAKE TWO ASPIRIN! *Traveling with Medicine*

It's always challenging traveling with prescriptions, but when you're recovering from an illness and have more drugs than usual, you really need to take some extra precautions to make sure you don't raise any red flags. The last thing you want is to end up at a destination without the prescriptions you need. Here's what you need to do to play it safe:

- Carry your prescriptions in your carry-on luggage.

- Bring more than you need in case your travels are delayed.

- Have a copy of your doctor's prescription with you.

- Make sure all prescription drugs are in clearly labeled containers.

- Make sure you factor any time changes in when taking regular drugs.

- Carry information about any allergic reactions the drug might trigger.

- Be sure the drug doesn't make you sun-sensitive—many do.

PAMPER YOUR SPIRIT
Spa Vacations

After you've recovered from an illness, your body may still need extra time to recuperate. The physical and emotional strain of fighting off what ailed you can take its toll. Even if you're mentally ready to climb mountains again, your body may have other ideas. Still, this doesn't mean you have to mope around your house in your pajamas watching soap operas all day. As long as you've been given the green light to travel, there's no reason why you shouldn't pack your bags and get a change of scenery. Getting out of the house should help lift your spirits and give you the opportunity to check out a new destination at the same time.

When your energy level is at an all-time low, a fantastic TRAVEL THERAPY option can be a spa vacation where the focus is on healing and rejuvenation. Where you decide to go can be as important as the kind of spa treatments you choose to indulge in, so here are three smart spa destinations where you can relax and unwind.

 DESTINATION: *Sedona, Arizona*

Arizona is one of the spa capitals of the world, and while there are dozens of award-winning spas in the Phoenix/Scottsdale area (see Chapter One), Sedona offers a unique spa environment where the emphasis is as much about spiritual healing as it is physical healing. At an altitude of more than 4,500 feet, Sedona often escapes Arizona's brutal summer temperatures, and the dry desert heat in the winter can help sooth aching bones. It's the perfect tonic if you're looking to escape a cold and damp environment.

This desert destination is known as one of the most revered healing places on the planet, and people come from all over the world to visit its vortex meditation sites. Because it's known as a spiritual capital, artists, healers, spiritual guides, and even intuitives have made Sedona their home, and many of them offer various services and classes.

Sedona is nestled among giant red rocks and has breathtaking scenery. There is a peaceful feeling that shadows you wherever you go in this quaint city, and life feels

slower and more deliberate, so it's the perfect place to let go and relax.

At Sedona spas, you'll find some unique treatments that you can't find anywhere else in the world because they were created to fit the "Sedona feeling," to help people find their inner harmony and balance.

One of the top spas leading the way in Sedona is the Mii Amo Spa (www.miiamo .com) at the Enchantment Resort. "Mii amo" means "journey" in the Yuman language, and a trip to this spa will leave you feeling like you've ventured into another world. Mii Amo spa is constantly ranked as one of the premier spas in the country, so you're in good hands when you sign up for a treatment here even if you're not exactly sure what that treatment includes. Like many of the spa treatments in Sedona, at Mii Amo the primary inspiration comes from the Native American culture. The stunning architecture of the spa is similar to ancient cliff dwellings, and as you enter the spa you'll notice

a wind-carved rock formation that's named Kachina Woman. Native Americans feel this is their Garden of Eden, a place where they believe the first woman gave birth to the human race.

When you're looking for a spa experience in Sedona, consider whether you want to just try out a day spa, or if you want a more intensive spa experience where you immerse yourself in the spa environment for several days. The best place for figuring it out is the Sedona Chamber of Commerce website at www.visitsedona.com. This website's spa listings are updated regularly, and you can also get a feel for the different resorts and restaurants in the area. There's a link to local activities as well, including hiking, horseback riding, and golfing. I think a scenic Jeep trip is a must if you truly want a feel for the Sedona area because four-wheeling in a Jeep, with an experienced guide, is a great way to learn more about the history of this very unique TRAVEL THERAPY destination.

DESTINATION: *Palm Springs, California*

For decades Palm Springs has been the playground of the rich and famous, but you don't have to be one of Hollywood's jet-set crowd

to appreciate the award-winning spas in this desert paradise. I first visited Palm Springs when I was going to college in Los Angeles. My friends and I were looking for a great weekend getaway that was close and affordable, so we jumped in the car and headed for

◀ *View of Cathedral Rock from Red Rock Crossing*
© KOR HOTEL GROUP

Palm Springs. While Palm Springs has some of the most luxurious accommodations you'll ever find, you can also find some bargain options. If you're looking for a spa experience, you can splurge by staying in one of the top resorts, or you can find a place that's more affordable, and just pop over to one of the fancy resorts to get your treatments.

One of my favorite spas in the Palms Springs area is at the famed La Quinta Resort & Club (www.laquintaresort.com). I took a close friend there for a bachelorette spa day, and it was an excellent choice. The serene

▲ *The Viceroy Palm Springs, Palm Springs, California*
© VICEROY PALM SPRINGS

setting and first-class service made it a day to remember. The Estrella Spa at the Viceroy Palm Springs (www.viceroypalmsprings.com) is also worth checking out. The Estrella even has a life coach on staff who offers special soul-searching sessions to their clients.

A good place to start researching which spa you want to bliss out at is the Palm Springs Bureau of Tourism website at www .palm-springs.org. This site offers a long list of local spas, along with the top places to stay, eat, and play. A perfect spa day could include indulging yourself with a few decadent treatments and then grabbing a quick bite to eat in one of Palm Springs many award-winning restaurants before doing a little shopping. If you want to completely chill, you can just stay at your spa all day long, doing nothing more than sipping refreshing drinks and catching up on your reading.

Palm Springs is easy to get to—only about 110 miles east of Los Angeles; and Palm Springs has a major airport. This desert oasis is blessed with fantastic weather year-round, boasting 350 days of sunshine a year. This is an ideal place to visit if you're in need of some "sun therapy" and want to chase the winter blues away. Even a day doing nothing more than lying by the pool and soaking up Palm Springs' relaxing atmosphere can do wonders for your disposition.

 DESTINATION: *Maui, Hawaii*

On my first visit to Maui, I was on a mission to find the most relaxing spa experience. On my quest, I crisscrossed this famous Hawaiian island and discovered that Wailea was a true spa mecca.

Wailea is on the southwest shore of Maui. It's a resort community that's known for its sensational beaches, friendly people, and lavish hotels. Back in the early 1970s, Wailea was only a patch of barren dirt, but local landowners decided to try and turn the area into a luxury resort haven, and the gamble paid off. While the spas you'll find in Wailea are very different from one another, their primary goal is the same: to capture the uniqueness that is Hawaii and incorporate the island feeling into the various treatments.

Taking top spa honors in the area are The Grand Wailea Resort Hotel & Spa, The Four Seasons Resort Maui, and The Fairmont Kea Lani; all have dazzling oceanfront properties that are continually creating unique spa experiences.

The largest of the three resorts, The Grand Wailea, has 780 rooms sprawled across forty acres and the largest spa in Hawaii.

When I first walked into Grand Wailea's spa, I felt like I was walking into a palace. It's huge and opulent. This is the kind of spa where you can easily spend the day because before or after your treatments you're invited to lounge in the Roman jacuzzi tub, and to try out the Japanese Furo bubbling bath, and even to sit underneath a cascading waterfall. Still, probably the most impressive option they offer are the five signature baths you can relax in. You'll want to try each one. They include a seaweed bath, a mud bath, an aromatherapy bath, a bath filled with papaya enzymes (my favorite), and a Hawaiian mineral salt bath.

Next to The Grand Wailea is a more intimate boutique spa at the fabulous Four Seasons. This award-winning Maui property bends over backward to cater to your every whim. You're even able to get some spa treatments poolside so you never have to leave the comfort of your cabana. It's pure bliss!

Right next to The Four Seasons, you'll find another top-rated spa at The Fairmont Kea Lani, Maui. You can try one of the many signature treatments at the spa or venture outside and have a treatment next to the pool. There are thirty-seven oceanfront villas at The Fairmont Kea Lani, Maui, that offer an exclusive spa menu, so when you

▲ *The Fairmont Kea Lani, Wailea, Maui, Hawaii*
© THE FAIRMONT KEA LANI, MAUI

stay in one of the villas you can have the ultimate private spa experience.

While a lot of people only try the spa where they're staying, Wailea is the perfect place to spa hop because these top three spas are right next to one another, with a short beachfront path connecting them all.

Throughout the island of Maui you'll find some amazing resorts and spas. If you want to venture outside of Wailea go to www.visit maui.com for some excellent insight. This website is run by the Maui Visitors Bureau and has a special link just for health and wellness that lists all the top spas on the island.

"After going through a difficult emotional period, my trip to Maui is just what I needed to help me clear my mind. I was blessed to enjoy a colorful, beautiful place that I will never forget. My experience in Hawaii has had a lasting impact on my life and I look forward to going back someday."

—THERESA PAIGE, FRONT DESK CLERK, NEW YORK

HOME AWAY FROM HOME
Vacation Home Rentals

You know the saying, "Home is where the heart is." But when you're healing from an illness, you've likely already spent too much time at home and the cabin fever is starting to set in. You need to get out and shake things up a bit. However, if you're not quite ready to deal with staying at a hotel or resort, then a home rental is a good choice because you can have everything you need close at hand but still feel like you're getting away on vacation.

There are dozens of ways to search for home rentals, but the first thing you need to do is to pick a destination. The idea behind a TRAVEL THERAPY home rental is to find a quiet and comfy home environment in a new place so you can venture out and discover new people, places, and things. When it comes to recovering from a stressful experience, I always find getting away to someplace quiet and laid-back is best. Finding a place where you can relax and still explore a little is key, which is why the following three Travel Therapy destinations were selected. Each one is on the beach, but that's where the similarities end. All three offer a completely different environment, from West Coast to East Coast. Pick the area that interests you most. Or you can choose a location that is the most opposite to where you live now so you can experience a new home away from home and broaden your horizons at the same time!

> "As an overconnected, overcommitted family, we rent vacation homes instead of staying at hotels to help us truly relax and unwind. We sit at the dinner table and just hang out and play games. It's a great way to catch our breath as a family and enjoy quality time together."
>
> —Brenda Collons, Advertising Executive, Washington

 DESTINATION: *The Hamptons, New York*

If you live on the West Coast, you're probably most comfortable and familiar with the beaches on the Pacific Ocean. That's the perfect reason to shake things up a bit and travel across the county to experience another coastline. If you've visited the East Coast before but you've never rented a place, keep in mind that there's a huge difference between staying a few days in a hotel and actually living in a home for a week or longer. When you rent, you become part of the community by doing simple things like going grocery shopping, going to the movies, and running other errands. Renting a home gives you a taste of what it would be like to live in a different environment, surrounded by new neighbors and a different way of life.

Renting a home and getting a taste for living in the Hamptons is one experience worth trying because this must-see destination is a beauty. The Hamptons are a legendary summer beach escape for people living in Manhattan and Connecticut. To clear up any confusion for outsiders, there isn't just one community called the Hamptons. The area is actually made up of a stretch of different towns and villages along the eastern edge of Long Island, about one hundred miles from Manhattan. Some of the most popular areas include East Hampton, where you'll find

Amagansett and Montauk, and Southampton, which includes Bridgehampton, Quogue, and Westhampton. Other popular favorites for vacation rentals include Sag Harbor, Shelter Island, Sagaponack, Water Mill, and Greenport. How do you decide which community to rent in? This might help: East Hampton is the ritzy area, where celebrities like Steven Spielberg are known to hang out, and where you go if money is no object. Areas like Southampton and Westhampton are popular for their laid-back vibe and convenience. Overwhelming, isn't it?

That's why your best bet is to spend some time online researching the different areas and then calling realtors in the places you're interested in so you can get a feel for pricing and availability. Another way to get quick information about rentals in the Hamptons is to go to www.vacationrentals.com, where properties from around the country are categorized and listed by area.

There are also several great websites to help you learn more about the different Hampton communities, including the site run by the Hamptons Visitors Council, www .hamptonsvisitorscouncil.com, and for insider information try www.hamptonstravelguide .com to hear what the locals are saying.

Insider tip: If you're even thinking about trying to rent during the popular summer months, be sure to reserve your spot early. The period between Memorial Day and Labor Day weekends gets booked up fast, so if that's the time you're thinking of traveling, you can't book your reservations too soon. Prices drop dramatically in the cooler winter months and the crowds have all gone home, so it's an amazing time to stay at the Hamptons if you can handle the chilly temperatures.

 DESTINATION: *Emerald Isle, North Carolina*

On my first visit to the Crystal Coast (on the southern outer banks of North Carolina), I was surprised by how beautiful the beach was. I'm not sure what I was expecting, but it certainly wasn't the marvelous miles of untamed coastline that I found in there. The next thing that grabbed my attention was how many different amazing homes were lined up along the beach. I was thrilled to find you can rent many of the homes for an affordable price, something that's rarely possible when talking about waterfront property. After exploring, the community of Emerald Isle turned out to be my favorite along the Crystal Coast.

What I like about Emerald Isle is that you feel very secluded in this quiet community, yet you're just a short drive away from several adorable towns and seaside villages. The area

also caters to children and families, which is why there are so many oceanfront cottages to rent that are family-friendly.

Renting a home on Emerald Isle is a special experience because you're able to stay so close to the water. With most of the waterfront homes, you only need to walk a few feet before your toes hit the sand. The views from these homes can easily keep you mesmerized for hours. Beachcombing is also fantastic here, especially if you go first thing in the morning.

It goes without saying Emerald Isle's sunsets are spectacular, so have your camera ready!

These beach home rentals are perfect if you're craving some privacy and want to escape the crowds. Even in the popular summer months, the crowds are nothing compared to the ones you'd find in Southern California or Miami Beach.

▲ *Home Rental on Crystal Coast, Atlantic Beach, North Carolina*
© CRYSTAL COAST TOURISM DEVELOPMENT AUTHORITY

If you're planning to rent on Emerald Isle, book ahead so you can get the best deal; also make sure you have a car so you can travel to the nearby towns of Beaufort and Morehead City. You also might want to check out Hammock Beach State Park, Hoffman State Forest, and the Cape Lookout National Seashore. For more on renting along the Crystal Coast check out www.crystal-coastnc.org, where you'll find lots of information about the area, and also try www.emerald islerealty.com.

DESTINATION: *Malibu, California*

For my senior year of high school, I left my home in Washington State and moved to Calabasas, California, to work as a live-in nanny so I could gain residency for college. It was a tough adjustment, made even harder by the fact that my route to Calabasas High School required that I face a fork in the road. If I turned left I'd get to the school; if I turned right, I'd go to Malibu Beach. I admit there were several times I couldn't resist the temptation and took the right and headed to the beach.

Since Malibu Beach was my first real California beach experience, it's fair to say I'm pretty spoiled. I was instantly impressed with Malibu's long stretch of beach. I loved watching the surfers trying to catch the next big wave. The homes along the beach are spectacular. I used to pick my favorite homes and promised myself that someday I would live in one. I was eighteen years old, but I remember those days at the beach like they were yesterday.

Depending on who you ask, Malibu either has twenty-seven or twenty-one miles of beach. It was twenty-seven before Malibu became an official city in 1991. Regardless, Malibu's beaches are some of the best in California, with popular favorites being Zuma Beach and Surfrider Beach. Hollywood A-listers quickly figured out Malibu's charm decades ago and started buying up oceanfront property there. The famed Malibu Colony is a gated community of multi-million-dollar homes and has included celebrity residents like Tom Hanks, Goldie Hawn, Barbra Streisand, Howie Mandel, Dustin Hoffman, Mel Brooks, and others.

While this colony is ultra-exclusive, there are a lot of other homes in the Malibu area that you can rent during the summer and winter months. Like any popular beach destination, you'll want to scout out your home early to make sure you have the best selection. You'll also need to decide if you can afford to stay right on the beach or if you're better off a few blocks away where the prices are more affordable. The best rentals in Malibu are snatched up fast, so if you see something you like, don't hesitate—grab it while you can!

Despite its popularity, Malibu still has its own distinct style and personality. The overall vibe is casual and laid-back and the shops and restaurants are more quaint than chic. Spending some time in Malibu should help you let go and relax and, if you find the right place to rent, this is an awesome TRAVEL THERAPY destination to help you build back your mental and physical strength. If you're looking for great weather to enjoy the beach, your best bet is staying in Malibu between May and October.

To learn more about the area, including some great information about local restaurants, hiking trails, beaches, and shopping, a good place to start is the Malibu Chamber of Commerce website (www.malibu.org) and the City of Malibu's website (www.ci.malibu.ca.us). Both websites offer of wealth of information and will get you on track to finding a home rental that's just right for you.

AUTHOR'S PICK

DESTINATION: *Jumby Bay, Antigua*

For a truly inspiring home away from home experience, Jumby Bay, a private island in the Caribbean just off of Antigua, is top on my list of TRAVEL THERAPY destinations for estate home rentals. To get to this exclusive escape, fly to Antigua and then take a private boat to the island. Only guests staying on the island are allowed to make the trip. This three-hundred-acre island houses a small resort and about a dozen multi-million-dollar estate homes that are for rent. This is a destination that is absolutely in the "splurge" category, but once you set foot in one of the estate homes you'll know why Jumby Bay is so special.

On my first trip, I stayed at Eagles Landing, an eight-thousand-square-foot privately owned beachfront home with five bedrooms, a workout center, a tennis court, and an infinity-edge pool that seemed to disappear into the Caribbean. During high season, this home rents for around $17,500 a night. It comes with its own butler, chef, and housekeeping

▶ *Oleander Estate Home at Jumby Bay Resort, off Antigua, West Indies*
© JUMBY BAY RESORT, A ROSEWOOD PROPERTY

staff. It was surreal. During my entire stay there I kept pinching myself to make sure I wasn't dreaming!

The island, along with the homes and the resort, is owned by the homeowners, though they've brought in Rosewood Resort to manage everything. The homeowners I've talked to say they started out staying at the resort and loved Jumby so much they decided to build their own homes there.

After touring several estate homes, I was curious about who lived in these million-dollar marvels. How often did they stay, and what in the world did they do to be able to afford this kind of luxury? I spent one afternoon at a tiny beach bar to find the answers. As it turns out, people from all over the world own homes on Jumby, including a lot of Americans and Europeans. Many are in the banking industry and most of them visit several weeks a year. Rosewood's MaryAnne DeMatteo, director of sales and marketing for Jumby Bay, says that most of the homes only get rented out for eight weeks out of the year and they are very selective about who they rent to. For a video tour of the different homes, check out Jumby Bay's website at www.jumbybayresort.com. You can also get an insider feel for the island and the homes for rent by logging into Jumby Bay's special blog at www.jumbybayblog.com.

What's truly special about staying in one of the homes at Jumby Bay is that you feel instantly comfortable, like you're a family friend. These homes are not set up as traditional rentals. They're private homes where the owners are sharing their slice of paradise with a few select guests. The homes are impeccably decorated and are ideal for anyone craving a luxurious escape.

Depending on the time of year, the cost for renting starts at around $5,000 dollars a night. If you find you don't need all that space, there are also lovely villas to rent in the $2,500 range that are all-inclusive.

Jumby Bay is the kind of place you come to decompress. Your main activities here will be lounging at the beach or pool, eating delicious meals, and sipping tropical cocktails. The quiet, lush, tropical surroundings force you to relax and rejuvenate, and when you're staying in homes this beautiful it's hard not to feel incredible and hopeful about the future. These homes are set up so you can bring family and friends or hold a special event, like a wedding, on the property. If you reserve during off-season and bring several couples, it will help cut down on the cost and you will be able to share in the magic that is Jumby Bay.

"Working in the travel industry, I'm lucky enough to have a job that allows me to travel to fabulous destinations and share things that I love about the place with people visiting for the first time. A perfect spot to watch the sunset, where to find the freshest fish around or the best bar for live, local music and great company . . . those are the things that give a place character and make you want to go back again and again."

—Kara Rosner, Account Executive Diamond Public Relations, Florida

Doctor's Orders Vacation Checklist

CHOOSE TRIPS WHERE YOU CAN

- Unwind
- De-stress
- Rest
- Catch up on sleep
- Gain your strength back
- Eat healthy
- Enjoy your surroundings
- Be inspired
- Rejuvenate

"We live in a wonderful world that is full of beauty, charm, and adventure. There is no end to the adventures we can have if only we seek them with our eyes open."

—Jawaharlal Nehru

Chapter 7

Celebrate

Whether you're a new mom wanting to rejuvenate with a pampering "Babymoon," or you're looking for a unique way to celebrate a promotion, graduation, retirement, birthday, or marriage, this is the TRAVEL THERAPY chapter for you! These picks are some of the best places to travel when you're looking to celebrate a special occasion.

It's easy when you're trying to plan a trip to fall into a rut and book the same vacation you always do because you know it's something you enjoy. Maybe you always go to Hawaii to celebrate your anniversary, or Mexico for a Girlfriend Getaway. Sure, it's tradition, but if you really want to celebrate a new milestone in your life, why not shake things up a bit and take a trip you'll always remember and create memories of a new place.

Here are some of the top TRAVEL THERAPY destinations to help you decide and get into the spirit of things. Don't forget the champagne!

- Baby Makes More—Babymoon Vacations
- Get Your Girl On—Girlfriend Getaways
- Honeymoon Havens—Romantic Escapes

Which destination suits you best? This time it's pretty clear-cut, depending on whether you're pregnant, ready to party with friends, or newly married. Still, take this fun TRAVEL THERAPY quiz and find out for sure.

◀ *The Big Island, Hawaii*
© HAWAII TOURISM AUTHORITY/KIRK LEE AEDER

TRAVEL THERAPY QUIZ

1 What song is on your mind?

a. "Babyface"

b. "Girls Just Want to Have Fun"

c. "I Honestly Love You"

2 You're thirsty for:

a. Nothing alcoholic

b. A cosmopolitan

c. A tropical umbrella drink

3 You feel like wearing something:

a. Loose-fitting

b. Sexy and fun

c. For the beach

4 You want to vacation with:

a. Someone who you can relax with

b. Your best girlfriends

c. Your husband

5 You are:

a. Ready for a Babymoon

b. Ready to party with your friends

c. Ready for a romantic escape

6 You want to go somewhere:

a. Quiet and calm

b. Exciting and new

c. Romantic

7 You would rather:

a. Go somewhere peaceful

b. Explore a new city

c. Relax on a tropical island

8 You're wishing for:

a. A healthy baby

b. An exciting Girlfriend Getaway

c. A romance to remember

TRAVEL THERAPY DIAGNOSIS

If you picked mostly "A" answers, then you're ready for a Baby Makes More Babymoon vacation where you can celebrate the huge life change that's coming and get some much-needed prenatal pampering. If "B" is your answer of choice, pack your bags and Get Your Girl On, because you need a Girlfriend Getaway that's out of this world. If you ended up with mostly "C" answers, then you'll want to look into the Honeymoon Havens TRAVEL THERAPY destinations where romance rules. No matter where you're going, remember this is a time to celebrate and be thankful for all you have. Cheers!

DESTINATIONS TO AVOID:

- Depressing destinations
- Stressful destinations
- Places that are nothing special
- Places that are not fun
- Uninspiring destinations
- Boring destinations
- Anyplace that is run of the mill

"'It's dark and hairy!' says the first one. 'No it's bright red and soft!' says the second one. 'What are you talking about? It is completely white and juicy!' says another one. Amazing how perspective can change when you go around a simple apple! Imagine going around the world!"

—DR. DANIE BEAULIEU, PHD, PSYCHOLOGIST AND AUTHOR,
LAC-BEAUPORT, QUEBEC, CANADA

BABY MAKES MORE
Babymoon Vacations

If you're pregnant and worried that once the baby is born you will never travel in the same way again, you need one last fling: Babymoon! Babymoons are one of the hottest new vacation trends, allowing expectant parents to celebrate their baby-to-be by signing up for some serious prenatal pampering. Babymoons are specifically designed to make sure your last vacation before your baby arrives is worry-free and full of unique surprises to help spoil both mom and dad.

Some of the most popular Babymoon destinations involve the beach, because the relaxing setting is the perfect backdrop for romance.

Some top sites to check out are Babymoon Guide (www.babymoonguide.com) and Babymoon Finder (www.babymoonfinder.com). Another Babymoon favorite is to head to a top spa where pregnant women are treated like royalty. For a great list of spas that have special prenatal offerings, try www.spafinder.com.

Although many doctors believe flying is safe during a pregnancy, be sure to check with yours before getting on a plane. All of the TRAVEL THERAPY destinations in this section are American destinations, so you won't have to travel too far. So what are you waiting for? The clock is ticking.

DESTINATION: *Phoenix/Scottsdale, Arizona*

The Phoenix/Scottsdale area makes a fantastic TRAVEL THERAPY destination for a Babymoon because this desert oasis specializes in world-class spas and hotels that take pampering to an entirely new level. Always on the cutting edge of any trend, Phoenix and Scottsdale also offer several resorts that have actual Babymoon packages, where all you need to do is sign up and show up with your baby bump—and everything else is taken care of for you.

One of the first hotels in the country to create a quality Babymoon package was the Westin Kierland Resort & Spa in Scottsdale. While some hotels just offer expectant parents a special rate and maybe throw in a massage, the Westin goes all out to help celebrate this monumental time in your

▶ *The Westin Kierland Resort & Spa, Scottsdale, Arizona*
© THE WESTIN KIERLAND RESORT & SPA

life. The Westin's Babymoon package aims to impress, and features a couple's massage and a goodie bag filled with all kinds of cool baby gifts (including $75 dollars in gift certificates). They also throw in an amazing in-room ice cream sundae station experience, complete with chocolate-covered strawberries. Still, my favorite over-the-top feature is the Westin's twenty-four-hour "Cravings Chef," who stands by to create whatever you crave. If you want some pickles with your ice cream, no problem, because the Cravings Chef has you covered! The Westin is also next to a huge outdoor shopping mall that's the perfect place to walk off all the calories you gobbled up at your sundae station.

Other resorts in the Valley of the Sun also offer special Babymoon setups, so you'll want to search around for the Babymoon package that pleases you most and then go for it. Two great sites to search are the Scottsdale Convention and Visitors Bureau (www .scottsdalecvb.com) and the Greater Phoenix Convention and Visitors Bureau (www.visit phoenix.com).

Insider tip: Unless you can handle the heat, it's best for expectant moms to visit the Phoenix/Scottsdale area when the temperatures aren't topping one hundred degrees. The best time for a Babymoon in this particular TRAVEL THERAPY destination is between October and April.

 DESTINATION: *The Big Island, Hawaii*

The first time I visited the Big Island of Hawaii I was impressed by the fact that I didn't feel overwhelmed by tourists. Unlike some of the other popular Hawaiian islands, the Big Island feels more like a secluded tropical paradise. The Big Island has some pretty impressive stats, too. Its Kilauea Volcano is one of the world's most active, and Mauna Kea is the world's tallest mountain, topping out at more than 33,000 feet when measured from its underwater base. The Big Island is famous for its coffee, macadamia nuts, and beautiful orchids. This is the perfect place to visit if you're searching for an authentic Hawaiian experience but want to escape the crowds. On the Big Island, you will find all the traditional beauty you would expect to find in Hawaii, along with some interesting side trips for the days when you want to do more than hang out at the beach. You'll also find some delicious restaurants in a variety of different price ranges that are sure to please any palate.

On the Big Island, you can also scout out some fantastic Babymoon and romance packages to help you celebrate this special time in your life. A smart place to start your search is www.gohawaii.com, where you can click on the link to the Big Island to find all the latest resort specials. You'll also find links that will bring you up-to-date on what's happening on the island and which different tours and travel deals are available.

What I like about the Big Island is that it's the kind of TRAVEL THERAPY destination where you can easily spend two weeks and never get bored. You can do as little or as much as you want, and you'll end up leaving the island feeling rested and rejuvenated, and ready to handle the new, exciting phase of your life that you're about to enter.

"After having our fifth child it was time to get away, just the two of us so we could recharge our batteries. We were only able to take a long weekend but it was enough just to get on the plane and not have to worry about all the kids and just be a little selfish and think about ourselves. Sometimes you just need a quick escape and to leave the place you live and get on a jet and fly away to a new destination. It was just what the doctor ordered!"

—TAMMY CARLIN, RESTAURANT OWNER AND MOTHER OF FIVE, GILBERT, ARIZONA

DESTINATION: *The Florida Coast*

The Florida coast, with its perpetually sunny skies and beautiful beaches, is an ideal TRAVEL THERAPY destination for a Babymoon because many of the hotels in the area offer special deals to help expectant parents feel at home. The last thing you want to do on a Babymoon vacation is worry about your comfort. The whole idea behind this celebration vacation is to take some time to be together and enjoy each other as a couple before the baby arrives and demands all your attention.

The point of a Babymoon is to catch up on your sleep so you can reserve all your energy and be in top form once the baby arrives. The beaches along Florida's coast, especially the less populated ones, can offer the inspiration and soothing environment you need for this last escape before your family changes for good.

One top choice is to head to the Ritz-Carlton on Amelia Island in Florida (www.ritzcarlton.com). This destination features quiet beaches and a chef that can handle any craving. There's even a Pregnancy Craving Menu, where you can get anything from ice cream and pickles to fruit smoothies. Amelia Island is often called one of the most popular beach destinations on the East Coast, so if you're looking to stay here, be sure to book as early as you can.

For more on what the Florida coast has to offer, go to the Florida Tourism website at www.visitflorida.com. Here you can click on the different areas of the Florida coast that you're interested in and find out which resorts offer the best Babymoon packages that fit your timetable and finances. The site gets updated often, so you can stay on top of the latest vacation packages and take advantage of the best deals.

GET YOUR GIRL ON
Girlfriend Getaways

Whether you're celebrating a birthday, graduation, or upcoming wedding, or you just want to escape with your best buddies to celebrate your fantastic friendship, a Girlfriend Getaway to the right TRAVEL THERAPY destination can be one of those life-changing trips you talk about forever. There's nothing like celebrating girl power to help fuel you forward and energize your inner spirit. On a Girlfriend Getaway, coming together is what matters most, and when you combine great friends with traveling to the right destination, you're destined for one fantastic experience!

When you're traveling with a group of friends, it's key that you all agree with the basic vacation plans so you don't have anyone whining halfway through, wrecking the trip for everyone else. This is all about coming together, not ripping each other apart. So have a basic idea of what the plan is so everyone can have the right mindset before you take off.

Whenever you're traveling with several people, there are bound to be disagreements. To help avoid any hassles before you leave, decide how you're going to deal with conflicts. Maybe you'll want to put things to a vote, or choose a group leader who will have the final say. Getting all this worked out beforehand should help ease any travel stress along the way so all you need to worry about is who's going to make the next champagne toast.

DESTINATION: *Manhattan, New York*

Manhattan is one of the sexiest and most stimulating Girlfriend Getaway destinations in the world. This is where you'll find the best of the best: the best in theater, art, dance, media, music, food, fashion, and finance. You name it and the top players are found in Manhattan. This is why this city is always sizzling with energy and excitement.

If you're coming to Manhattan, you have to bring it. This is not a TRAVEL THERAPY destination you want to pick if you're looking for some quiet time to sit around a pool and catch up with your friends. On the contrary, Manhattan is the city you pick if you're ready to hit the town running and never slow down. Think *Sex and the City*. If a day of window-shopping along Madison Avenue sends chills down your spine, and the thought of catching the latest Broadway play seems like the perfect way to start out an evening, then Manhattan has you covered. You can be in the city a week and not even scratch the surface because there is so much to do and see. In fact, you can live in Manhattan and still not

▲ *Triplex Penthouse at New York Palace Hotel, New York*
© NEW YORK PLACE HOTEL

experience everything because things change so fast it's almost impossible to keep up.

You can come to Manhattan just to experience the world-class museums, like the Museum of Modern Art and the Metropolitan Museum of Art, or plan a trip around the theater, ballet, opera, and symphony, or you can hit all the top tourist attractions.

If it's your first visit, must-sees include: the Empire State Building, the Statue of Liberty, Rockefeller Center, Times Square, Central Park, Wall Street, Broadway, and at least several of the different neighborhoods like Soho and the Upper West Side.

Manhattan is a great place for women traveling alone or in a group because it's relatively safe and convenient. You don't need a car to navigate around the city—all you need to do is hop on the subway or hail a cab. And the popular perception that New Yorkers are unfriendly is a myth. I've found the opposite to be true. Before I moved to the city, I'd often get turned around trying to find my way around town, but there were always people happy to help me out.

Traveling to Manhattan takes some preparation if you want to save some money and get the best prices. Airfare changes all the time, so be sure to do your research and get the best deal. Always compare prices, since New York is served by three different airports.

You also never want to pay full price for a theater ticket without first checking for discounts at reputable online sites like www

.broadwaybox.com, www.playbill.com, and www.theatermania.com. These sites often offer discounts up to 60 percent off on top shows like *Wicked, Jersey Boys, Hairspray, Chicago, Legally Blonde, Mamma Mia!,* and others. This is a great way to go if you don't want to stand in line the day of a performance trying to get last-minute discount tickets. With these sites you can reserve ahead, so you know you have your tickets and won't miss the show you want to see. Discounts aren't usually offered for the newest, most popular shows, so if you have your eye on a particular one, book early from the theater where the show is playing.

The average room rate in New York City is close to $300 a night, so it also pays to shop around for the best price and take advantage of any specials. If you want to celebrate your time with your friends in style, some TRAVEL THERAPY favorites include the elegant but hip New York Palace Hotel (www.newyork palace.com), the funky and fun Empire Hotel (www.empirehotelnyc.com), and the luxurious classic Four Seasons Hotel, (www .fourseasons.com/newyorkfs). One of the smartest things to do before you pick your hotel is to decide what area of the city you want to focus on during your visit because that's the area where you'll want to stay. If your trip is centered on the theater, shopping, or eating then you'll want to find a hotel in the neighborhood where you have access to those priorities. It doesn't do you much good to get a cheap hotel on the East Side if everything you want to do is in Midtown Manhattan.

Finally, be sure to pack some comfortable shoes because you'll be walking more than you can even imagine. One insider tip during summer is to wear flip-flops when you're walking around at night and to carry your cute strappy sandals in your big oversize purse. Before you go into a club or restaurant you just make a quick swap and you're good to go! Also, be sure to rest up before you come because Manhattan truly is the city that never sleeps—and you don't want to miss a moment!

BARGAIN BABY! *Travel Deals*

Places like Europe, New York City, Florida, and Hawaii are destinations where you can find some great deals on airfare and hotels if you're willing to do a little research. Here's a list of some of the top websites that can help you search for travel bargains. Spending a few minutes surfing these special sites can save you hundreds of dollars!

- Kayak.com—Airfare deals
- Airfarewatchdog.com—Airfare deals
- Hotwire.com—Discount airfare deals
- Priceline.com—Hotel discounts
- Hotels.com—Hotel discounts
- Mobissimo.com—Discounts on international travel
- Luxurylink.com—Discounted travel packages
- Orbitz.com—Deals on airfare, hotels, rental cars
- Homeexchange.com—How to home swap

Be sure to check the airlines you're flying to see if they offer any package deals. I've saved a lot of money combining airfare and hotel deals. Not only is it much cheaper, but you also avoid all the extra taxes. If you have frequent flyer miles, check to see if there are any special bonuses or incentives for cashing in those miles before you book your flight.

The general rule of thumb is never pay the first price you find. A little digging will usually get you a better deal. Then you get the vacation you want, and you save a little money at the same time!

DESTINATION: *Europe*

My first visit to Europe was for a two-month stay, and the only luggage I had was my backpack. It was both liberating and a little scary, because I was only twenty-one and had never really traveled outside the United States, except to take quick trips to Mexico and Canada. I had researched Europe for months and I had a tentative plan of where I wanted to go so I could see as much of the different countries as possible in the eight weeks I had. Funds were tight, so I was relying on staying in guest homes. I've always liked the idea of living with locals in their homes because it gives you a real feel for the people in the country you're visiting.

This trip changed the way I travel. After Europe, I'd never again settle for a "regular" vacation in the States. If there was any way I could hop on a plane and explore a new part of the world, I was on it. I also learned you don't have to be rich to travel, as long as you're smart and research the best deals ahead of time.

Europe is an ideal TRAVEL THERAPY destination for a Girlfriend Getaway because there are so many things to do that no one can complain about getting bored. One fun idea is to have everyone in your group pick the place they'd most like to see and put them in charge of researching that specific spot. Then, when you get to your destination, that person is the "tour guide" and the expert for that part of the journey. This gives everyone a chance to research and visit their desired location and also be able to lead the group. Another option is to pick one person in the group who's the expert traveler and designate them as the group leader, so they're in charge of making the most of the travel arrangements after talking to everyone about what people want to see.

If you plan to travel extensively through Europe, you can often save a substantial amount of money by buying an unlimited train pass, called a Eurail pass. This way, depending on how long you're going to travel, you pay one price up front and you're able to go wherever you please, whenever you want, and change your plans on the drop of a dime, and still have your transportation covered. For more on rail passes, go to www.eurail.com.

There are hundreds of travel books about Europe, but for the most current information your best bet is to go online to a site like www .visiteurope.com, where you can check out all the newest specials and travel trends. You can also search other sites online and pull from your favorite travel books to make a guide that's tailor-made for your trip.

When going to Europe, be sure to shop the airline specials because prices can change drastically. Also, consider flying into London instead of Paris because when you arrive, jet-lagged and exhausted, it's nice to be in a country where they speak English in case you need any help getting around.

I always advise to let someone back home know your itinerary, and to check in every so often. It's just a smart thing to do in case you run into any trouble. Also, be sure to make a copy of your passport and stash it somewhere else in your backpack so if your original passport gets stolen you still have all the information.

> *"Before I got married, I wanted to have one last trip of freedom. So I set off to Europe with three girlfriends and one backpack. At the age of twenty-six, it was a great way to travel and take some time to look into my own life before taking the plunge into married bliss. Not only that, it allowed me to learn how to throw caution to the wind and realize you still end up with two feet at the end of the day."*
>
> —ANGELA AN, REPORTER, COLUMBUS, OHIO

 DESTINATION: *Paris*

I've been fortunate enough to visit Paris a handful of times—with boyfriends and girlfriends—but I have to admit that I enjoyed my girlfriend trips the most. With my best gal pals, I was able to spend hours checking out designer shops, lingering at museums, strolling along the Seine, and sipping wine at outdoor cafes.

There's no doubt Paris is one of the most romantic cities in the world, but it can also be a spectacular Girlfriend Getaway, where you and your friends can focus on things like spending the day at a fantastic spa or shopping for shoes. Paris is one of the fashion capitals of the universe, so even if you're not a big shopper, or if your funds are limited, it's still an amazing experience to spend the day with your girlfriends window-shopping at famed stores like Gucci, Hermès, Christian Dior, Yves Saint Laurent, and Versace.

If you're itching to buy something "Parisian" but you don't want to max out your credit card, Paris has several flea markets, where, with a little patience, you can discover some spectacular one-of-a-kind outfits.

One of my favorite things to do in the City of Light is to sit at an outdoor café at sunset and enjoy a lovely glass of Bordeaux with friends. You can catch up on life while you soak in the intoxicating Parisian scenery.

To help you narrow down what you'd like to do on your visit to Paris, go to the official website of the French Tourist Office (www.francetourism.com). This site offers a comprehensive overview of the country along with some specific suggestions about visiting Paris. The Paris Convention and Visitors Bureau has a website that's more specific to Paris at, http://en.parisinfo.com, so check there as well.

Regardless of how long you're staying in Paris, some top experiences you shouldn't miss include the Eiffel Tower, Notre Dame, the Arc de Triomphe, the Louvre, the Musée d'Orsay, Montmartre and Sacré Coeur, the Latin Quarter, Château de Versailles, and taking a cruise along the Seine.

HONEYMOON HAVENS
Romantic Escapes

There's no better time to celebrate than after you say "I do" and you're officially ready to start your life together as a married couple. I've heard friends say that a wedding, no matter how wonderful, is one of the most stressful events you'll ever be a part of, so it only makes sense to pick a fantastic honeymoon to help you regroup and revitalize.

For most people, planning a wedding is exhausting, so the best Travel Therapy honeymoon havens involve romantic escapes that are as far away from your regular life as possible. You want a honeymoon that you'll remember, a fantasy trip that highlights the love you have for each other.

This is a time when it's okay to splurge. During your marriage there will be plenty of chances to go for the cheaper options, but your honeymoon shouldn't be one of them. Even if money is tight, there are other areas you can cut back on so you're able to take the special honeymoon you both deserve. Don't panic, splurging doesn't have to mean spending thousands and thousands of dollars, but it does mean you have to select a destination that inspires you both, one you've always wanted to go to but never had the opportunity.

◄ *The Seine at night, Paris, France*
© DMITRIY KOVYAZIN

When you're planning your trip, make sure you take the extra time to research and choose a vacation that will rock both your worlds. Get ready to consider three world-class TRAVEL THERAPY destinations that offer a little something extra.

> *"For our honeymoon we wanted to go somewhere special so we headed to Machu Picchu in Peru and words and pictures can't do the destination justice. It's a spiritual space that can only be experienced while being there. Machu Picchu possesses this aura of peace and tranquility, fragments of my Peruvian heritage and remnants of a civilization long gone. You go there to find yourself and lose yourself in its ambience."*
>
> —DELIA CAMASCA, SENIOR RECRUITER, NEW JERSEY

 DESTINATION: *Santorini, Greece*

The island of Santorini, Greece, is one of the most visually beautiful islands in the world. It's a true honeymoon haven to remember. The first time I saw Santorini was by boat and I must have taken at least fifty photographs trying to capture the heart of this picture-perfect destination.

When I was a teenager, I saw a movie that was shot on Santorini, and I was so inspired by the scenery that I waited until the end credits to find out where the movie was filmed. When Santorini came up, I scribbled it down in my notebook and promised myself I would visit that island someday. It took me about ten years, but I finally made that dream come true, and I found Santorini even more amazing than I'd imagined. I was a broke college student at the time, so I couldn't afford to stay anywhere fancy. I toured the area and decided someday I would be back to stay in one of the grand whitewashed villas that are perched high on Santorini's cliffs, overlooking the Aegean Sea.

As a honeymoon destination, Santorini has all the ingredients to inspire romance and relaxation. This unique, out of the way, secluded, exotic, and breathtakingly beautiful island charms you from the moment you arrive. If you come by sea, one of the first things you'll notice is a staircase built into the side of the island that crisscrosses all the way to the top to Santorini's capital city of Fira.

To get to Fira, you can take a cable car up the side of the cliff or you can walk up the five hundred-plus winding steps, or opt for the more traditional option of riding on the back of a donkey. No matter how you journey, the scenery along the way is fantastic, so be sure to have your camera ready.

For the ideal TRAVEL THERAPY experience, visit Santorini during the early spring or fall to avoid the crush of the summer crowds. Staying in Santorini sans tourists is the only way to get a real feel for this Greek gem. If possible, you'll also want to stay in a cliff-side resort or private villa where you can immerse yourself in the magic of the Cycladic architecture. Some of the most romantic and luxurious hotels on the island are:

- Mystique (www.mystique.gr), with eighteen exclusive suites and villas

- Perivolas (www.perivolas.gr), which has one of the most beautiful pools on the island

- Canaves Oia Hotel (www.slh.com /canaves), featuring transformed 17th-century cave houses overlooking the Aegean

- Villa Katikies (www.katikies.com /santorini-villas), a villa with seven units on a cliff overlooking the sea

- Kirini Hotel (www.kirini.com), where you can book the ultra-romantic Honeymoon Suite or Kirini Suite

For more ideas on where to stay, and for information on private villa rentals, check out www.santorinigreece.net and www.santorini luxuryhotels.com.

DESTINATION: *Virgin Gorda, Caribbean*

The island of Virgin Gorda in the British Virgin Islands is a magical place for a honeymoon because of its exclusive and remote location. This is the place to pick if you want to escape the usual tourist traps, because on Virgin Gorda you'll find only a few small luxury properties. The island itself has quite a history. Christopher Columbus named the island because he thought it resembled a fat woman lying down. Thus its namesake: "Fat Virgin."

On the north side of the island, you'll find the Bitter End Yacht Club. This lively resort is a favorite for couples and families looking to enjoy some water sports. For a more secluded and luxurious feel, you'll want to head over to a resort called Rosewood Little Dix Bay (www.littledix-bay.com). The grounds are gorgeous, the service is impeccable, and the beaches are quiet and beautiful. Add this to the fact that Little Dix also has an award-winning spa and

amazing restaurants, and you've just found your own little slice of heaven.

Little Dix Bay's original resort was designed in the 1960s by Laurance S. Rockefeller, with the idea of creating an exclusive private escape. Today, even with one hundred-plus rooms, you rarely see many guests because of the layout of the property. I remember finding the beach practically empty during my stay there and later discovering that the resort was completely booked.

If you're looking for a romantic couple's spa treatment, don't miss the Cliff Spa Suite, where the view is breathtaking and every detail down to the candlelight is perfection.

Where Little Dix has a more sophisticated atmosphere, Biras Creek (www.biras.com), the other top romantic resort on the island, has a more rustic feel. With only thirty-one suites, Biras Creek is tucked away on a 140-acre peninsula, so you genuinely feel like you're lost in paradise when staying at this award-winning honeymoon destination. Each suite has two bicycles out front, and you quickly learn that's pretty much the only way to get around the property because there are no cars. Even if you take a wrong turn, you won't get lost for long because almost every dirt road eventually leads to the water.

One of the things that make Biras Creek so special is that you have the Atlantic Ocean on one side of the property and the Caribbean on the other, so you have your pick of different beach environments, depending on what you're looking for. The Caribbean side offers an ideal place for swimming, sailing, and snorkeling, and you can also sign up for special dive trips. The Atlantic is more untamed and rugged. It's the perfect place to relax on the beach and watch the waves roll in.

The vibe at Biras Creek is laid-back and peaceful so you can soak up the sun and explore the property at your own pace. You might spot another couple at the beach, but generally this resort is so large that you feel like you have the entire grounds to yourself. What better way to start a romantic life together!

◀ *Villa Aquamare, Virgin Gorda, BVI*
© KAREN SCHALER

DESTINATION: *Bora Bora, French Polynesia*

You've probably seen pictures of Bora Bora, because this stunning French Polynesia TRAVEL THERAPY destination is often featured in magazines and on television as a honeymoon hot spot! Bora Bora is where you'll find those charming overwater bungalows and thatched roof villas suspended on stilts over a turquoise lagoon. It's not an exaggeration to say the luxury properties on this island look like they're straight out of a fairytale.

Because Bora Bora is one of the most dramatic and romantic islands on the planet, it's no surprise that the properties here cater to couples who travel from all over the world to soak up the amazing ambience. For more than four decades, Bora Bora has shared its unique beauty with travelers who come here to unwind and rejuvenate. Catching a sunset from your own private deck or slipping into the crystal clear water right outside your front door is an experience like no other. The resorts on this island know how to spoil people, so much so that you won't want to leave.

The hardest thing about this TRAVEL THERAPY destination is deciding which fantastic property to book. While the high-end luxury resorts get the most attention from honeymooners, Bora Bora offers unique places to stay—even if you're on a budget. You can actually camp on the island if you're looking for that kind of experience.

To help you sort through all the selections, head straight to the official Bora Bora tourism website at www.tahiti-tourisme .com. This website is full of pictures that will make you want to hop on a plane immediately! Another good site to try is called Bora Bora Island, www.boraboraisland.com. Here you can find hotels in all price ranges.

Some of my favorite picks for honeymooners include:

- The Four Seasons Resort Bora Bora: www.fourseasons.com/borabora
- Bora Bora Lagoon Resort & Spa: www.boraboralagoon.com
- Le Meridien Bora Bora: www .starwoodhotels.com/lemeridien
- Hotel Bora Bora: www.amanresorts.com /hotelborabora
- The St. Regis Bora Bora Resort: www.starwoodhotels.com/stregis
- Sofitel Bora Bora Motu: www.sofitel.com

If you end up falling in love with Bora Bora, you might want to check out some of the other superb islands that make Tahiti—officially known as French Polynesia—such a honeymoon hot spot. There are more than one hundred different islands in the area, but standout favorites include Moorea, Taha'a, and Huahine.

▶ *Overwater bungalows at Le Meridien, Bora Bora, French Polynesia*
© LE MERIDIEN, BORA BORA

AUTHOR'S PICK

DESTINATION: *Mallorca, Spain*

After a week in Paris, one of my best girl-friends and I decided to spend a weekend in Mallorca, an island in the Mediterranean Sea just off the coast of Spain. We had heard Mallorca had some fantastic nightlife, along with some beautiful beaches, so it sounded like the perfect Girlfriend Getaway. We didn't have the funds to stay anywhere spectacular, but we found a lot of affordable options just a few blocks from the beach outside of Palma de Mallorca.

Mallorca boasts three hundred days of sunshine a year, but we happened to choose one of the few rainy days. We were just getting settled on the beach when it started pouring, so we have hilarious photos of us standing in our bathing suits in the soaking rain at a vacant beach. During the downpour, we headed into town to take shelter and checked out some cute shops and restaurants along the way. Thankfully, it didn't take long for the sun to come out so we were back at the beach in no time.

After dinner our first night, we set out to find some of the island's fabled night-life. It was about ten o'clock, and we were disappointed to find everything closed. We couldn't believe it! We had heard so much about the "party life" on Mallorca. Completely confused, we eventually settled on a tiny, quiet bar that had a few locals in it. By two in the morning we were tired and ready for bed, so we headed back to our hotel and were shocked to find the clubs and bars that had been closed earlier were now just opening up and people were lining up to go inside. The entire atmosphere had changed to fun and festive. After talking to a few partygoers, we realized our mistake. In Mallorca, the hot spots don't open until very late, or very early depending on how you look at it, and they stay open until breakfast.

Our final night in Mallorca, we had a blast staying out until the sun came up and walking back to our hotel around the same time we'd usually hit the beach. There is something so decadent about staying up all night; it makes you feel like you're getting away with something. It's also exhausting, so if you're going to Mallorca for the party scene, rest up and be prepared to sleep during the day so you can party with the best of them all night!

For more on where to stay and sights to see in Mallorca, go to the official tourism site for the Balearic Islands (www.illesbalears.es).

Mallorca has more than fifty beaches, so think about beach hopping and staying in different hotels along the way.

Also, when you're searching for deals, keep in mind Mallorca has variations on its spelling. Be on the lookout for Majorca as well as Mallorca.

"I've seen the positive impact travel getaways make for women. They get together for fun, bonding, and friendship and go home nicer wives, mommies, and friends!"

—Nadja Piatka, Founder of Ultimate Girls Getaway,
Buffalo, New York

Celebrate Vacation Checklist

CHOOSE TRIPS WHERE YOU CAN:

- Celebrate
- Be inspired
- Love life
- Create amazing memories
- Spend time with people you care about
- Be pampered
- Escape stress
- Explore new places

"*No amount of travel on the wrong road will bring you to the right destination.*"

—Ben Gaye III

Chapter 8

Lost And Found

When you've experienced the loss of a loved one or dear friend, it can feel like a freight train has run over your heart, leaving you shattered, empty, and exhausted. Other major losses can also leave you heartbroken—like losing a job that was part of your identity, or even leaving friends behind to move to a new town. These are the types of experiences that can zap the energy and inspiration right out of you. Unfortunately, there's no magic salve to help ease your pain, but when you're ready to take that first step and move forward, going on the right trip can help you down the road to recovery.

Often, when you've suffered a major loss, there's a tendency to hide away and isolate yourself because you just don't have the strength to deal with the outside world. But becoming a recluse will only make your situation worse. As hard as it might be, you really need to surround yourself with other people and saturate your life with activity.

To help give you a nudge in the right direction, TRAVEL THERAPY has three different destinations ideas to help you after a loss:

- Follow the Leader—Unique Group Tours
- Come Sail Away—Cruises
- Relax, Everything's Included—All-Inclusive Vacations

Which trip is right for you? Just take the easy TRAVEL THERAPY quiz and you will be one step closer to seeing how travel can help you heal.

◀ *Biking in Denmark*
© DENMARK TOURIST BUREAU/DITTE ISAGER

TRAVEL THERAPY QUIZ

1. How physically fit are you?

   a. Very, love to exercise

   b. Not very, where's the buffet?

   c. Average, would rather lounge

2. You are up for:

   a. Trekking or biking

   b. Kicking back on a cruise

   c. Relaxing at the beach

3. The thought of being on a ship for a week:

   a. Freaks you out, you need your space

   b. Sounds heavenly, sign you up

   c. You'd rather be at a resort

4. You would like to pack:

   a. Biking or hiking shoes

   b. Boat shoes

   c. Resort shoes

5. Group tours:

   a. Can be fun if the tour's interesting

   b. You'd rather relax than tour on foot

   c. No thanks, where's the hotel?

6. I want to travel:

   a. Outside the United States

   b. Anywhere on a cruise

   c. Someplace warm with a beach

7. I would like to go away:

   a. For a week or two

   b. Indefinitely

   c. For a short time

8. I don't mind eating:

   a. On the run

   b. At a buffet

   c. Resort food

TRAVEL THERAPY DIAGNOSIS

If "A" is your answer of choice, then you're ready to move on with your life, literally. The vacation destinations under Follow the Leader include unique TRAVEL THERAPY group tours that will challenge you not only physically, but mentally, too. If "B" is the answer you picked the most, then Come Sail Away will help you get ready for smooth sailing on some fantastic TRAVEL THERAPY cruise destinations. If you ended up with mostly "C" answers, then pack your resort wear and head to one of these TRAVEL THERAPY all-inclusive resorts. These Relax, Everything's Included vacations are all about helping you find places where you don't have to worry about a thing because these world-class properties have you covered!

DESTINATIONS TO AVOID:

- Couples-only destinations
- Places where you can hide out
- Places where you visited as a couple
- Places where you're not around people
- Places where you aren't active
- Honeymoon havens
- Romantic destinations
- Isolated destinations
- Quiet destinations

"If you rule out the airport part of travel these days, I recommend travel for my clients. Therapy is all about getting out of rigid mental states, leaving the same old, same old behind. Travel stirs the pot. One feels and experiences something different in their body and le voilà: The impossible becomes possible!"

—MICHELE RITTERMAN, CLINICAL PSYCHOLOGIST AND AUTHOR, BERKELEY, CALIFORNIA

FOLLOW THE LEADER
Unique Group Tours

The first thing that comes to mind when I think of a "group tour" is a crowd of people packed on a bus, all wearing tacky T-shirts and following someone who's carrying a sign with the group's name on it. Yuck! Of course, I know there are many wonderful and unique group tours out there that don't even come close to this negative description, but in case you have similar concerns, know that I avoid these kinds of tours and would never steer you in the wrong direction.

The beauty of a good group tour is that you are surrounded by people from all walks of life. Everyone has different experiences to share, and even if you don't like a particular person or two, being in a group environment can help take your mind off your own troubles. So even if you feel like avoiding people like the plague, put yourself out there and open yourself up to new experiences and friendships. You might be surprised by what you find.

The goal of this TRAVEL THERAPY is to choose a unique and exciting destination that would be hard to explore on your own, so you actually need a group tour to make sure you have the right experience and don't miss anything. The following three TRAVEL THERAPY options go above and beyond to make sure your group adventure is something special.

 DESTINATION: *Denmark*

There's something magical about visiting places that seem like they're plucked right out of a fairytale. Denmark is one of those destinations, and from the moment you arrive it's easy to see why famed author Hans Christian Andersen drew such inspiration from his home country. Denmark is one of prettiest places I've ever visited. While Copenhagen is the most popular city, with the biggest tourist attractions (The Little Mermaid statue and Tivoli Gardens), the entire country impresses with its gorgeous scenery. One of the best ways to appreciate the landscape is by taking a bike tour. You can rent a bike and take off on your own, but with so many first-rate tours offered, you miss out if you choose the solo route, especially since the tours give such insight into Denmark's glorious history. The best tours keep their groups small and offer unique off-the-beaten-path side trips. You can pick a tour that only lasts a few days, or go for it and sign up for a two-week trip—or even longer. It all depends on the time and budget you have and how much of the country you'd like to see. A word of warning, though: Once you start doing bike tours, they can get addicting. The endorphins from the exercise start kicking in and you'll wonder why you ever traveled any other way. Having the wind in your face and amazing scenery all around you does something to your spirit. You'll be left feeling exhilarated and inspired.

For help on selecting the best bike tour, the Denmark Tourist Bureau (www.visitden mark.com) has some great links to get you started. The folks at the bureau say biking is one of the best ways to experience Denmark, and there are a dozen different routes highlighted on their website that cover every corner of the country. Denmark supports its bike tours with great signage throughout the country, so you can't go wrong no matter where you choose to explore.

I also found it very helpful to go over some insider tips on the website before signing up for a trip. Some of the smartest advice includes:

- Village churches are good landmarks along your route and always have toilet facilities.
- Draw your planned route on a map with a transparent marker so you can still see where you're going.
- Protect your maps by keeping them in plastic folders.
- Don't let a fixed schedule ruin your chance of having spontaneous moments en route.
- Limit your luggage to a minimum; you can buy en route if needed.
- Buy an extra lock—a wire padlock—to keep your bike safe.
- Many old inns offer accommodation with plenty of atmosphere.
- Danish youth and family hostels are extremely comfortable.
- Get a wing mirror for your bike to keep track of the traffic behind you.

 DESTINATION: *Austria*

I lost my heart to Austria when I saw *The Sound of Music*, and on my first journey to this charming country I headed straight for Salzburg, where a majority of the movie was filmed. What I found was a city even more enchanting than I expected. I spent as much time as I could walking and hiking around the area just absorbing the atmosphere.

When I heard about a walking tour where you get to venture from Innsbruck to Salzburg and play golf in between, I knew it was a winner. A group called the Wayfarers runs this unique tour. This tour operator has been around for several decades and specializes in walking adventures all over the world.

This Austrian tour is rated as "moderately difficult" and combines spectacular sightseeing with some unforgettable golf greens. On this one-week adventure, you walk between seven and eleven miles a day on well-groomed mountain paths and through grassy meadows. The group leader is an accomplished golfer, so you get all kinds of great insider information about the area and how to play the different courses you come across.

If you love the idea of a Wayfarers walking adventure, but you're not a golfer, Wayfarers offers more traditional walks in dozens of destinations. To get the latest schedule, go to their website at www.thewayfarers.com. Chances are you'll find yourself spending hours on this site because the featured trips are so captivating. I talked to a handful of people who have gone on a Wayfarers trip and say they enjoyed their first walking tour so much that they now sign up for walking tours every year to explore different parts of the world on foot.

"To walk in the countryside of Austria is so invigorating, with the fresh mountain air and beautiful scenery. It looks like it's out of a movie. The views are clear and colorful, the wildflowers bloom all season, the cowbells and church bells ring in the distance. The Austrians are warm and friendly, and you'll encounter local people on foot, going about their everyday business but wanting to share it with you. This is the only way to experience Austria."

—MICHAEL WEST, CO-FOUNDER OF WAYFARERS, DORSET, UNITED KINGDOM

 DESTINATION: *Mongolia*

Mongolia is one of those mysterious places you usually don't hear a lot about. It's far enough off the tourist track to make it an ideal TRAVEL THERAPY destination for an adventure tour. Part of the adventure is getting there;

then you get to discover this country's unique culture. If you book a trip to Mongolia, don't be surprised if your friends and family look at you a bit confused and ask why. Most people aren't even sure exactly where this country

is, much less have any idea about what this interesting part of the world has to offer.

Because Mongolia can be a challenging country to navigate, it's smart to sign up for a group tour and let someone else worry about the travel plans. One of the standout tours is offered by Nomadic Expeditions (www .nomadicexpeditions.com).

The tour is called From Yak to Kayak and for about two weeks you venture through Mongolia exploring the wilderness by—you guessed it—everything from a yak to a kayak. Seriously!

Stops include Lake Hovsgol and the Gobi Desert, and besides riding on a yak and in a kayak, horse trekking through the Khoridol Saridag Mountains is also on the agenda. This trip also includes hiking through the Yol River Valley and checking out the sand dunes of Moltsog Els. One of the many highlights is visiting the famous Flaming Cliffs where it's said the first dinosaur eggs in the world were discovered.

▲ *Touring in Mongolia*
© THREE CAMEL LODGE, MONGOLIA

This is a fascinating tour on so many levels. The experience is so all-consuming that you won't have any time to dwell on your loss or worry about your future. In Mongolia, you learn to live in the moment, like the nomads who still roam this country. The tour only allows about a dozen people, so the feel is exclusive and intimate, and you'll connect with other travelers and share your experiences.

Along the journey you stay in a variety of places. On some nights you'll sleep in a hotel; on others in traditional *gers*. Gers are nomadic tented homes that are popular among the Mongolians. They're convenient because when you're ready to move to a new location you can literally pick up your home and take it with you.

A trip to Mongolia will make you feel like you've stepped into a scene from *Arabian Nights*. If you want to visit Mongolia but aren't ready to "yak and kayak," you can find some alternative touring options, and get information about the different areas of the country, by going to the official Mongolia Tourism website at www.mongoliatourism .gov.mn. On this site, you'll also find some interesting history about the role of tourism in Mongolia.

COME SAIL AWAY
Cruises

After my father went through a difficult loss, he decided to go on a singles cruise. At first I was a bit nervous about it because I wasn't sure he was ready to jump back into the game so soon. I went shopping for some "cruise" clothes with him, and he was so animated and excited that I decided this trip would do him a world of good. My father doesn't travel often, so it was a big deal for him to make such a large commitment to a vacation. I was proud of him for taking the plunge, and the stories he came back with made me realize how a cruise can do wonders to help cheer you up and change your attitude after a loss.

Many people pick a cruise when they want to travel to several different locations but don't want to worry about how to get from point A to point B. On a cruise vacation, you are literally chauffeured from destination to destination. All you need to do is sit back, relax, and enjoy the ride!

There are so many cruise options to pick from that it can get a little mind-boggling. To help you sort through all the choices, there's a super website, Cruising (www.

cruising.org), that's run by a nonprofit group called Cruise Lines International Association (CLIA). CLIA represents two-dozen cruising companies, and it's also involved in developing health and safety guidelines to help make sure your cruising experience is top-notch. A quick check of CLIA's website will let you know which cruise lines travel to the specific destination you're looking for with links to those companies.

> "When my father died years ago, his ashes were spread over the mountain ranges of Alaska, the place he loved above all places. Decades later, to remember him and ease our pain, I flew my mother and me to Alaska. We rented a small plane and flew over the same mountains where my father's ashes were spread. It was an emotional but very fulfilling and calming journey."
>
> —KATHY BEZOLD, RETIRED, PORT ORCHARD, WASHINGTON

 DESTINATION: *Alaska*

Growing up in the northwest, Alaska has always held a special fascination for me. I had many friends when I was younger who moved to Alaska for the summers to work on fishing boats or in the canneries to help earn money for college. The pay was good, but in most cases it was the adventure and the stunning landscape that brought them back to Alaska year after year.

With its rugged beauty and remote location, Alaska is another part of the world that's challenging to tour on your own. You can do it if you have a lot of time and money, but cruising is a smart way to get an effortless overview of this huge chunk of wilderness. Alaska covers more than 570,000 square miles and is twice the size of Texas, so it's not the kind of place you can simply fly into and get around easily. Then, of course, there's the weather you need to deal with, so that's why taking a cruise is a smart choice.

Some of this destination's highlights include the mountains and awe-inspiring glaciers; it is also a wildlife haven, so it's not unusual to see huge grizzly bears, moose, caribou, and bald eagles. Be sure to have your camera ready. If you don't have a zoom lens, it might be a good time to invest in one because you don't want to miss a shot and be kicking yourself later.

Because there are so many different cruise lines offering trips to Alaska, it's a good idea to research the areas you want to visit and then pick a cruise that makes stops in those places. Most of the cruises take off from Vancouver, British Columbia, or Seattle, Washington. To start your research, go to Travel Alaska (www.travelalaska.com), where Alaska's tourism division has created one of the most gorgeous travel websites I've ever seen. The beautiful photographs will inspire you to brush up on your own photography skills. You'll also find detailed information about Alaska's many amazing destinations, as well as some great links to things to do, where to stay, and what to eat. Some of the top cruise lines with Alaska itineraries include:

- Regent Seven Seas Cruises: www.rssc.com
- Princess Cruises: www.princess.com
- Celebrity Cruises: www.celebritycruises.com
- Cruise West: www.cruisewest.com
- Carnival: www.carnival.com
- Royal Caribbean International: www.royalcaribbean.com
- Holland America Line: www.hollandamerica.com
- Norwegian Cruise Line: www.ncl.com

Also keep in mind that because of the obvious weather restrictions, the cruising season in Alaska only runs from about May to September. If you're looking to book a trip, be sure to do it early so you're not left out in the cold!

 DESTINATION: *Greek Islands*

The first time I explored the Greek Islands, I was going the budget route, so I was thrilled to find my Eurail pass included free ferry rides to the islands. It sounded like the perfect deal until I found out that my free ride was a deck seat, which literally means sitting on an open deck. This would have been a cool way to travel if I hadn't picked an overnight trip. Brrrrr! Still, traveling by boat—with stops at the islands of Corfu, Mykonos, Santorini, and Ios—was an amazing way to experience the islands. Seeing the islands from the water also gives you a great overall feeling for the area because each island is so different.

A more comfortable way to visit a lot of islands quickly is with a cruise. Then you can always go back and spend more time on your favorite island. Most major cruise lines depart from the port of Piraeus in Athens. To check out destinations, visit the Greek Tourism website at www.greek-tourism.gr.

The website has links for different hotels all across the Greek Islands and also lists each island separately so you can scroll through and see which one jumps out and grabs your interest.

After you decide where you want go, your next step is to look into which cruise line fits what you're looking for. Some top choices on the TRAVEL THERAPY list include:

- Seabourn Cruises: www.seabourn.com
- Silversea: www.silversea.com
- Crystal Cruises: www.crystalcruises.com
- Orient Lines: www.orientlines.com
- Norwegian Cruise Line: www.ncl.com
- Costa Cruises: www.costacruises.com
- Windstar Cruises: www.windstarcruises.com

Folks who get a little wobbly on the water enjoy cruising in this part of the world because the seas are usually calm and the weather ideal. If you're looking for some quality down time and just want to relax and avoid the crowds, the best time to go cruising in the Greek Islands is in the spring and early fall. If you're craving some exciting activity to help take your mind off things, you might want to consider cruising during the summer months of July and August when the usually peaceful Greek Islands turn into party central.

▲ *The famous churches at Oia (or Ia) on Santorini*
© PAUL COWAN

 DESTINATION: *Mexico*

With more than four hundred beaches, Mexico is one of the top cruising destinations in the world. There are so many interesting ports of call in this country that you would have to take several cruises before even scratching the surface.

I've traveled to more than a dozen Mexican destinations, but I still feel like I've only experienced a tiny fraction of this fascinating country. Before booking your cruise, it helps to narrow down the area of Mexico you'd like to visit and then pick a cruise that focuses on what you're looking for. One of the most popular cruising stops is Cozumel, and other hot spots include Manzanillo, Mazatlán, Puerto Vallarta, Los Cabos, and Cancun. These popular ports can get pretty crowded, so if you go ashore you might want to venture away from the usual tourist traps and find a cute place to sip a margarita and enjoy more authentic surroundings.

▲ *One&Only Palmilla, Cabo San Lucas, Mexico*
© KAREN SCHALER

To learn more about Mexico, the country's tourism board has put together a comprehensive website that's packed full of all kinds of helpful information at www.visitmexico.com. There are close to two-dozen primary cruise lines offering cruises to Mexico, so you will have a lot to choose from. Some top-rated cruise lines to check out include:

- Royal Caribbean International: www.royalcaribbean.com
- Regent Seven Seas Cruises: www.rssc.com

- Silversea: www.silversea.com
- Windstar Cruises: www.windstarcruises.com
- Oceania Cruises: www.oceaniacruises.com
- Holland America Line: www.hollandamerica.com
- Crystal Cruises: www.crystalcruises.com

Insider tip: Even if you don't speak any Spanish, saying hello (*hola*) and thank you (*gracias*) will go a long way in Mexico. I've always found the people there to be extremely friendly, and they seem to honestly appreciate it when you try to speak their language.

> "A few months after my second brain surgery (I was eighteen), I went on a trip to Mexico with my mom's best friend and her family. Newly bald again and feeling very self-conscious I ended up on the trip with a swimsuit that unbeknownst to me had become very see through. I was horrified but ended up meeting someone and having an innocent vacation romance that helped me get over being bald very quickly!"
>
> —KIMBERLY PAPPAS, PUBLIC RELATIONS, SCOTTSDALE, ARIZONA

RELAX, EVERYTHING'S INCLUDED
All-Inclusive Vacations

There's nothing worse than going on vacation and getting nickel-and-dimed to death, spending way more than you ever imagined or budgeted for. All those secret hidden fees and taxes can zap the fun right out of your trip really fast. This is where an all-inclusive vacation can save you big bucks. Every time you eat or order a drink you don't have to worry about how much it's going to cost because you've already paid up front. Most of the top-rated all-inclusive properties don't even allow you to tip the hotel staff, so you truly can leave your wallet at home. The idea behind choosing an all-inclusive destination is to indulge in a worry-free vacation.

There are certain parts of the world that have perfected the all-inclusive idea, so you're not stuck with nasty buffet food and cheap alcohol. The goal of a successful TRAVEL THERAPY trip is choosing a destination, figuring out how much you're comfortable spending, and then being able to pay up front so you can spend your time focusing on enjoying yourself. An all-inclusive vacation is ideal because you can relax and not worry about how much everything is costing you.

One word of warning: Be careful and make sure you read the fine print when selecting your all-inclusive property so you know exactly what's included in your package price. Some all-inclusive resorts charge extra for certain water sports and premium alcoholic drinks. Depending on the focus of your trip, pick the place that includes everything you're looking for and then kick back and enjoy!

 DESTINATION: *Dominican Republic*

This untamed island is a fantastic choice if you're looking for an all-inclusive trip with a jungle feel and secluded beaches. The Dominican Republic is the new kid on the block when it comes to tourism, and many properties are opting to go the popular all-inclusive route. The island is full of cultural and ecological wonders and the beaches seem to stretch on forever. Different areas of the island have distinctive vibes, so check out www.godominicanrepublic.com to find the top all-inclusive properties on the island that have what you're looking for.

If you're craving a luxurious setting, you'll want to check out The Bungalows (www .thebungalows.com). When the property opened in April 2008, it was the first all-inclusive five-star resort in the Dominican Republic. Tucked away on Confresi Beach in Puerto Plata, this adult-only all-inclusive resort offers the ultimate peaceful escape. Here you'll find delicious gourmet meals and a world-class spa. It's a 108-room resort that's designed to help people unwind and forget about their worries.

If you want to explore this country, the Ministry of Tourism recommends whale watching, horseback riding, kayaking, four-wheeling, helicopter rides, caving, and golf. Even just driving around to the different beach communities is an enjoyable way to spend some time. The all-inclusive resorts are

set up to cater to your every whim, though, so if you're looking for some downtime, all you need to do is unpack your bathing suit and sunscreen and let the de-stressing begin.

DESTINATION: *Playacar, Mexico*

Throughout the country of Mexico you can find a plethora of all-inclusive resorts, but for world-class service and top-of-the-line amenities you'll want to head to the beach community of Playacar. It's only a forty-five minute drive south from Cancun, just outside of Playa del Carmen in the Yucatan Peninsula, in the area known as the Riviera Maya.

Top on the list of all-inclusives is the award-winning Royal Hideaway (www.royalhideaway.com). What I appreciate about this AAA Five Diamond winner is its emphasis on quality and service. There are several gourmet restaurants on the property, and all your beverages—including top-shelf cocktails and wine—are included. It's an adult-only resort, so you don't have to worry about screaming children and shrieking parents ruining your vacation bliss.

▲ *The Bungalows Resort, Dominican Republic*
© THE BUNGALOWS RESORT, DOMINICAN REPUBLIC

If you've ever held a bias, and I admit I had one, about cheap, all-inclusive resorts in Mexico, The Royal Hideaway will change all that. You're handed a glass of champagne upon arrival—my idea of a great start to any vacation! The Royal Hideaway is just one example of why Playacar is a smart TRAVEL THERAPY destination. To look into some other resorts in Playacar, go to www.visitmexico .com and www.playacarallinclusive.com. Both of these websites allow you to research the various all-inclusive options and to learn more about the Playacar area. Also, keep an eye out for special deals as all the resorts run regular discount packages and travel incentives throughout the year.

 DESTINATION: *Antigua, West Indies*

When I was invited to an all-inclusive resort in the Caribbean I had my doubts. At that point I was still in my phase of believing that all-inclusives meant nasty cold buffet food and overcrowded pools. I decided a long time ago I'd rather skip a trip than go someplace cheap and disappointing. When I was assured there was nothing "cheap or disappointing" about some of the all-inclusives on the island of Antigua, I decided to give it a shot. Still, I didn't get my hopes up.

To say I was blown away by the quality of many of the all-inclusive resorts on Antigua is an understatement. On Antigua, they bring all-inclusives to a whole new level. The word *cheap* doesn't even come close to describing these resorts. To stay here you'll need to dig deep into your pocketbooks, but the experience is worth every penny!

First thing's first: Antigua has 365 beaches. The tourist office likes to joke there's a beach for each day of the year. All of the beaches are open to the public, so all you have to do is pick an area you like the best. Chances are, though, if you're staying at an all-inclusive you won't even leave the resort.

One of my favorite properties on Antigua is Curtain Bluff (www.curtainbluff.com). This legendary resort has been around for decades and always wins top honors as an exclusive luxury retreat. With only seventy-two rooms, its emphasis is on making you feel like family. All your meals, drinks, and water sports are included, and you're asked not to tip—so you don't have to worry about how much things cost. The one thing that isn't included are trips to the spa, but don't let that stop you because this spa is a showstopper! It's built right into a cliff overlooking the Caribbean and offers some decadent treatments that bring new meaning to the concept of relaxation.

For other all-inclusive properties on Antigua, start with the Antigua and Barbuda Department of Tourism website at www.antigua-barbuda.org. Also, when you're looking at prices, don't shy away if things initially look a little pricey. Don't forget that your meals and drinks are included, as well as water sports and all resort taxes. If you factor in what all that would cost separately, your all-inclusive price is usually a real bargain.

If money isn't a worry and you're looking for the ultimate splurge, one of the top-rated all-inclusive resorts in the world is just a ten-minute boat ride from Antigua. This celebrity favorite resort is called Jumby Bay (www.jumbybayresort.com) and it offers a private island experience like no other. (For more information on this resort, see page 148.) To up the ante even more, the resort had a major overhaul in 2008, which included adding new rooms, a new pool, and a luxurious spa. This private island is three hundred acres, and you can stay at the main resort or rent your own private villa or estate home.

▲ *Curtain Bluff Resort, Antigua*
© DIGISHOOTER

If you're going through a time in your life when you're dealing with a loss, you need to be prepared for those random moments when you're overcome with emotion. No matter how strong or positive you are about moving forward it's only natural to experience these difficult feelings. To help you through the rough patches here's a checklist for a TRAVEL THEARPY survival kit to take with you on your trip.

- A journal to write down your feelings
- The number of several friends you can call that will always listen
- Kleenex
- Visine
- Aspirin
- Waterproof Mascara
- A list of ten positive reasons you wanted to take this trip

AUTHOR'S PICK

DESTINATION: *Dachau, Germany*

Whenever I'm feeling down or fighting off feeling sorry for myself, there's nothing like a good dose of reality to put things into perspective. When things go wrong in life, it's easy to ask the question, "Why me?" But instead of getting sucked into that cycle of self-pity, I like to throw myself into a difficult experience so I can remember just how lucky I really am.

This TRAVEL THERAPY attitude has propelled me to work in two war zones, and while I can't recommend either as a travel destination, I can recommend visiting places that give perspective and appreciation for what we have.

I was only a college student when I visited the Nazi concentration camp at Dachau. I wasn't prepared for the intense feeling of sadness and remorse that flooded over me when I saw the life-size photographs of the prisoners. These men and women suffered so much, and being there in the presence of those images and seeing the looks in their eyes drove home just how massive and horrific the Holocaust atrocity really was.

After visiting this concentration camp-turned-memorial, I vowed to never take my life for granted, and to try to make a difference and help people who couldn't help themselves.

That visit to Dachau is one of the reasons I decided to work as a television news reporter covering soldiers' stories while embedded with the troops in Bosnia and Afghanistan.

There are many amazing and inspiring places in this world to visit. This is my pick because I feel there's nothing comparable to experiencing a slice of human history—including some of our most tragic moments.

This kind of TRAVEL THERAPY may not be the best choice for everyone who is still struggling with depression while going through a difficult transition in life, but if you're the type of person who finds strength in looking outside your own pain, this is the type of trip that might put what's happening in your world into a different perspective. Empathizing with others who have lost so much often allows us to be more thankful for what we do have and what we've experienced so far in our lives.

If you would like to visit Dachau (www .kz-gedenkstaette-dachau.de), you can get there from Munich in about twenty minutes. The memorial is open every day except Monday, and you'll need at least three hours at the site. You can visit Dachau on your own, but for a better understanding of what went on there between 1933 and 1945, a guided tour is best. This visit is sure to stir up painful feelings, but it may also empower you to move on and, if you're lucky, find your own way to make a difference.

Lost And Found Vacation Checklist

CHOOSE TRIPS WHERE YOU CAN:

- Heal emotionally and physically
- Relax and unwind
- Forget about your problems
- Enjoy your time away
- Create positive new memories
- Meet new people
- Learn about new destinations
- Interact with different cultures

"Two roads diverged in a wood, and I—I took the one less traveled by, and that has made all the difference."

—ROBERT FROST

Chapter 9

Reinvent

*I*t starts with a feeling. You know deep inside that it's time for a change. The same old routine isn't working anymore. If you're ready to take the plunge and reinvent yourself, the possibilities are endless! What you need is an inspiring TRAVEL THERAPY vacation to help you find your new fabulous self.

Maybe your kids have recently left home and you're left alone wondering what you're going to do with the rest of your life. Or maybe you've finally moved on from a toxic relationship that was sucking the life out of you and holding you back. Or perhaps you're at a place in your career that feels like a dead end and you know there has to be something more for you out there. Whatever your reason for wanting to reinvent yourself, just do it! You've earned the right. You deserve it. Go ahead, book a TRAVEL THERAPY trip and don't look back.

Here are three smart options to help you find the new you—the person you've always wanted to be!

- Culture Shock—Unique Destinations
- Table for One—Solo Travel
- Lesson Learned—An Old Dog *Can* Learn New Tricks!

How do you decide which trip is best? Just take this fun TRAVEL THERAPY quiz and get ready for your life to change!

◀ *Exploring Schilthorn outside of Interlaken, Switzerland*
© KAREN SCHALER

TRAVEL THERAPY QUIZ

1. You're looking to:
   a. Explore someplace exotic
   b. Travel alone
   c. Learn something new

2. Thoughts on traveling alone?
   a. Maybe, depends on where
   b. Yippee, sign me up!
   c. Sure, if I'm in a group setting

3. You're ready to:
   a. Travel someplace completely different
   b. Spend some time with yourself
   c. Pick up a new skill

4. You want to:
   a. Be challenged culturally
   b. Go solo for this journey
   c. Learn something fun

5. Your thoughts on learning a new language?
   a. Cool
   b. Maybe
   c. Would rather not

6. When it comes to food:
   a. You'll try anything
   b. You keep it simple
   c. You want to make it yourself

7. How much time do you want to travel for?
   a. Several weeks
   b. One week
   c. A week or less

8. You would rather go:
   a. Off the beaten path
   b. By yourself
   c. With an organized event

TRAVEL THERAPY DIAGNOSIS

If you picked mostly "A" answers, then you're ready to venture to an exotic location where you'll be plunged into an entirely different culture. Learning about different people, places, and things helps you learn about yourself in the process—and that's the ultimate reward. If "B" is your answer of choice, then you need some one-on-one time with yourself. On solo trips, you can listen to what your heart and head are saying so you can come home refreshed and revitalized and ready to make a change. If you found yourself picking mostly "C" answers, then you're all set for a learning vacation, where the focus is on doing something you've never done before. The empowerment you'll get from conquering a new skill will stay with you long after you return home, so try it! You won't regret it.

DESTINATIONS TO AVOID:

- Places you always go to
- Typical tourist traps
- Destinations crowded with Americans
- Places you've been to before
- Couples only destinations
- Places devoid of culture
- Uninspiring destinations
- Destinations that aren't challenging
- Places where there's nothing new to learn

"Going to a new place breaks you out of your rut and forces you to use new parts of your brain. It makes it easier to interrupt old, bad, ingrained patterns. If you're in a stuck spot in your life, go alone to someplace you've never been. You will meet the 'new you' there!"

—JANE FENDELMAN, COUNSELOR AND AUTHOR, PHOENIX, ARIZONA

CULTURE SHOCK
Unique Destinations

Sometimes the best way to shake things up is to travel to a destination that's completely different from what you're used to. I'm talking about the kind of place where you get off the plane and instantly think, *Wow! We're not in Kansas anymore.*

From the climate to the people to the food and the culture, this kind of TRAVEL THERAPY vacation can open your eyes to a whole new world. Immersing yourself in a completely different environment allows you to jump-start your imagination and climb out of the rut you've been living in. With a fresh perspective, you'll be able to reevaluate that same old safe life of yours that's been boring you senseless.

There's a reason for the phrase "culture shock." If you've never been far from home, and you haven't experienced different ways of life, traveling to a new country can be overwhelming at first. You need to prepare yourself mentally and physically and open your mind and your heart to having a new experience.

If you choose one of these trips, things are going to be very different from what you're used to at home—and that's the whole idea. You're trying to get away from what you know and broaden your horizons. Keep in mind that no matter how much you research, read, and prepare yourself for a different culture, there are still things that are going to catch you off guard. Embrace the differences. Cherishing those moments that challenge your perceptions is how you grow. Adapting to a new culture isn't always easy, but if the idea of challenging yourself by visiting a different part of the world and learning about a new culture gets your adrenaline pumping, then there's no better way to reinvent yourself than traveling to a unique destination where you can soak up sights, sounds, and smells. It's hard to imagine a new way of life when you're completely consumed by the one you're living. So take the chance and discover something completely unique—and you could end up discovering a lot about yourself in the process.

 DESTINATION: *Dubai*

Dubai is the Las Vegas of the Middle East, and that alone makes it a fascinating TRAVEL THERAPY destination. Though it's true that both destinations have casinos, the real comparison comes in Dubai's ultra-futuristic, flashy architecture that lights up the skyline at night. Everything is bigger than life, and spending time in Dubai can help jump-start your creative juices and get you thinking outside the box.

Dubai is a city of contrast. In one corner you'll find some of the most structurally spectacular buildings in the world, while in another you'll find camel races. It's the blend of old and new that makes Dubai one of the most interesting tourist destinations in the world. This country is everything you'd expect and more—with a few surprises thrown in just to keep you on your toes.

The city of Dubai sits right on the Persian Gulf, and ever since oil was first discovered there in 1966, Dubai has been on the development fast-track and has never looked back.

▲ *The Palm Mall, Palm Jumeirah, the Palm Islands, Dubai*
© THE NAKHEEL COMPANY

At times, a visit to this country can seem very metropolitan. You'll find yourself shopping in designer shops and eating gourmet meals. However, traditional Muslim customs are in full effect here, which means no drinking alcohol outside of hotels and licensed clubs.

One of Dubai's most surprising activities is Ski Dubai, the Middle East's first indoor ski resort. Other suggested sites to see include the Grand Mosque and the Dubai Museum. Hands down, though, Dubai's biggest draw is the tax-free shopping. Your credit card is going to get some exercise here because you can buy many name brand items cheaper than you can at home. Some of the best shopping is at Dubai's Palm Islands, which are gigantic manmade islands off the coast of Dubai that have been dubbed by some as the eighth wonder of the world.

While no trip to Dubai would be complete without checking out some of the spectacular hotels, you need to get outside the luxury zone to get a taste of the true Dubai. A great place to start researching your journey is at the Department of Tourism and Commerce Marketing website at www.dubaitourism.ae. Here you can check out all the hotels and restaurants and also look at what cultural side trips are available. You'll also find some helpful information about what you can expect in terms of safety and cultural differences. You want to make sure when you're traveling to Dubai that you're heading to this destination with your eyes wide open. You'll also want to save up money for this trip because Dubai is notoriously expensive. But keep a close eye out for great deals, because they certainly can be found.

 DESTINATION: *Malawi, Africa*

Malawi is one of the poorest countries in Africa, where HIV/AIDS have left hundreds of thousands of children orphaned. Despite this devastation, Malawi is an amazing place to visit. The Malawi people are known as some of the friendliest in the world and one of the first things you'll notice when you arrive is how genuinely happy the Malawians are. I quickly learned that even though the way of life in Malawi is difficult by U.S.

standards, this is the only life the Malawian people know, so they don't waste time complaining.

Malawians have mastered the art of living each day to the fullest. In a country where salesmen line the street selling coffins, people talk candidly about not knowing if tomorrow will come for their family, friends, or even themselves. I was reminded in Malawi to live each day like it's your last, and to never put

off something you really want to do because that day may never come.

Even with its extreme poverty and health crisis, Malawi is a visually beautiful country. One highlight is Lake Malawi, the third largest lake in Africa. This massive lake is more than 360 miles long and 50 miles wide, covering about a fifth of the country. It's a popular spot to visit because you can find all kinds of simple resorts and small hotels up and down the lake. Some good choices include:

- Safari Beach Lodge: www.safaribeachlodge.net
- Club Makokola: www.clubmak.com
- Ntchisi Forest Lodge: www.ntchisi.com

One of my personal favorite TRAVEL THERAPY resorts in the country is the Mvuu Safari Camp (http://malawi.safari.co.za), which is located in southern Malawi in the

▲ *On Safari in Liwonde National Park, Malawi, Africa*
© KAREN SCHALER

Liwonde National Park. The camp is right on the Shire River. A river safari, where you pass dozens of hippos lounging in the water, is one of the many highlights. You feel like you're on the Jungle Cruise ride at Disneyland, only when these hippos wiggle their ears, it's for real! Because the camp is right on the river, don't be surprised if you wake up and find a hippo sleeping in the grass just off your front porch. It happens all the time.

At this all-inclusive camp you can also do game walks and regular driving safaris. When I was there, we tracked down a herd of elephants and were able to drive right up to them for some amazing photographs. Unlike other areas of Africa where the safari experience involves dozens of other people racing around in Jeeps, in Malawi you feel like you're in the middle of nowhere and it's just you and the animals.

Malawi has only recently started marketing itself as a tourist destination and the tourism bureau says it has high hopes that more people will discover this unique African experience. A simple website has been set up at www.malawitourism.com that will help give you an idea of what the country has to offer. There's also an email link there so you can send any questions you might have. The Internet in Malawi is not always fast or reliable, so you need to be patient when you're looking up websites. If they don't work at first, check back. Chances are the Internet was just down the first time.

Like any country with health issues, you'll want to be sure to get the proper immunizations before visiting. The Center for Disease Control and Prevention (www.cdc.gov) is the best place to start. The CDC has a special link dedicated to travelers' health. Click on the country you're visiting and get up-to-date information about how to protect yourself. For Malawi, you'll probably be advised to take malaria pills, and be sure to talk with your doctor to find out exactly what you need before getting on the plane.

"A trip to Cambodia with my fifteen-year-old son altered the course of my life and business. After visiting a country that inspired me so much, I decided to start two nonprofit organizations as a way to give back. My leap of faith to go somewhere totally unplanned resulted in the best experience of my life. The connections I have made because of that impulsive decision continue to multiply to this day, allowing me to try and make a difference in other people's lives."

—THERESA HINES, FOUNDER OF ONE PEARL, FARMINGTON, CONNECTICUT

DESTINATION: *Vietnam*

The two primary places people usually want to visit when they head to Vietnam are Hanoi, the capital, and Ho Chi Minh City (formerly Saigon), the largest city in the country. Both cities offer a lot to see and do, but if you're going to make the journey halfway around the world to Vietnam, try to get out and see some of the countryside while you're there. Experiencing the less populated areas in Vietnam gives you a more authentic feel for this country and its people.

To help you journey outside the usual tourist hot spots, the Vietnam National Administration of Tourism has put together an easy-to-navigate website (www.vietnam tourism.com) with information covering the entire country, from where to stay to what to see to information about Vietnam's culture and history. Vietnam is a country where you can find everything from beautiful beaches to impressive mountain peaks, so take some time to consider the type of trip you want to have and then go from there.

Like any country that has gone through a war, the scars run deep in Vietnam. Though the Vietnamese are generally very warm toward Americans despite the troubled history between the two countries, it goes without saying that you want to be respectful of this country's history. In Vietnam you can learn lessons about forgiveness, letting go of the past, and moving forward to a better future.

When you're looking to experience cultural differences, Vietnam is a perfect place because there are more than fifty ethnic groups living in the country. Now that's diversity! The country borders Cambodia, Laos, and China, and all of their cultures create a melting pot that's part of what makes Vietnam so special.

Speaking a few words in Vietnamese goes a long way here. To help you navigate this culture, here are some specific rules of etiquette you should follow so you don't offend anyone. They include:

- Don't stand with your hands on your hips.
- Don't point with your finger or gesture with your hand.
- Don't cross your arms in front of your chest.
- Don't touch a member of the opposite sex.
- Don't shake hands if you are a woman.

It's always smart to read up on the rules of etiquette for any country you're visiting before you leave because you never know when a simple gesture that's perfectly acceptable in the United States is considered quite rude in another country. Better safe than sorry!

Before you travel, make sure to check out the U.S. Department of State's website (www.state.gov) and look for any travel or

health warnings for Vietnam. Sometimes they post things like avoiding traveling too close to the border, where U.S. citizens have been known to be detained. But don't let these types of warnings deter you from visiting the country. It's important to keep things in perspective. It would be like researching the United States and finding out it's not smart to wander along the Arizona/Mexico border and then canceling your trip to New York.

When you're traveling to foreign countries, it's important to know what you're getting into before you go so there aren't any unpleasant surprises. Being prepared in case something unforeseen happens is just traveling smart so you can enjoy your adventure to the fullest.

◀ *The Cai Be Floating Market on Mekong River in Vietnam*
© EMILY LOH

BE SMART! *Foreign Travel Tips*

If you're headed off to a foreign country, you want to make sure to take care of some key things before you go so you're protected. Just follow this simple TRAVEL THERAPY checklist and you'll be good to go!

- Call your credit card company to let them know you're traveling so your card isn't shut down after the first foreign transaction.

- Check with the CDC website (www.cdc.gov) about any immunizations you might need.

- Make sure you have the required paperwork, including visas and proof of immunization.

- Make a copy of your passport and important credit cards and carry it somewhere separately in case your passport gets stolen.

- Bring over-the-counter anti-diarrhea and indigestion medicines.

- Know some basic words in the language of the country you're visiting.

- Give your itinerary to family or friends at home.

- Check in with your cell phone company about making international calls.

- Register with the embassy in the country you're visiting at www.state.gov.

- Find out about Internet access before you leave if you're planning to email.

- Read up on the cultural etiquette in the country you're visiting.

TABLE FOR ONE
Solo Travel

Traveling alone and knowing that you can go anywhere you want, whenever you want, and that nothing or no one can stop you is one of the most empowering things you can do. You're in charge of your own destiny and you don't have to get permission or acceptance from anyone else. It's also a huge confidence booster to know you're okay traveling alone, eating solo in a restaurant, or sightseeing by yourself. To go on a solo vacation you have to be open to the idea of having new experiences and meeting new people. When you travel with an open mind, the possibilities are endless.

The first time I went on a major trip by myself, I immediately noticed how self-conscious I felt. I got on the plane and kept looking around at everyone else. All I could see were couples traveling together, or groups of families and friends. There didn't seem to be anyone else who was traveling alone. I felt the same way the first time I ate at a fancy restaurant alone. It just felt weird. It took some adjusting, but once I stopped worrying about what other people were thinking, the power of solo journeying (and eating alone, for that matter) kicked in.

When you're traveling alone you're practically forced to interact with new people. When I travel solo I meet more new friends and interesting people than I generally do when I'm traveling with someone else. When you're by yourself you're not only more open to talking to strangers, but you also aren't distracted by the restrictions of a travel partner. Traveling alone allows you to absorb your surroundings and trust your instincts, which might mean changing your itinerary at the last minute and following the path that feels right to you.

It takes guts and courage to go on a vacation by yourself, but the payoff is tenfold. You want to make sure you pick a destination that inspires you, maybe someplace you've always wanted to go but could never find anyone to go with you. This is your chance to have it all. It's your call. It's intoxicating to know you're in charge of your own destiny and that anything is possible!

DESTINATION: *Zihuatanejo, Mexico*

I like to head to Mexico for a quick weekend escape when I'm craving some culture but don't have the time to venture halfway around the world to find it. When it comes to solo travel, Zihuatanejo is a special destination that's top on my TRAVEL THERAPY list because of its off-the-beaten-path location and safe and easy to get to.

Zihuatanejo is a sleepy little fishing village nestled along the Pacific Ocean, and it looks like something out of a postcard. Actually, it *is* out of a movie. A strip of Zihuatanejo's idyllic beach was the backdrop at the end of *The Shawshank Redemption*.

What makes this Mexican destination so special is its authenticity. Zihuatanejo isn't overflowing with tourists or tacky T-shirt stands. There are no high-rises or fancy malls or American fast food restaurants. Zihuatanejo is the real deal—a small Mexican beach community that's as charming as it is relaxing.

If, after a few days of R&R, you're looking for some nightlife to spice things up a bit, venture down the road a few minutes to neighboring Ixtapa. Where Zihuatanejo is known for its quaint hotels and peaceful setting, Ixtapa has a thriving hotel zone and bustling bar scene. The two cities are only a few miles apart, but they couldn't be more different.

I prefer to stay in Zihuatanejo because you can spend the day relaxing on the beach sipping margaritas. You can also stroll into town and check out some small markets that cater to the locals. Zihuatanejo is also safe for solo travelers, and it's refreshing to visit a place where you aren't bombarded by souvenir stands.

In Zihuatanejo you'll find places to stay across all price ranges, but you shouldn't miss looking into the award-winning Tides resort (www.tideszihuatanejo.com)—at least for

one night. At the Tides Zihuatanejo, there's a casual, chic vibe that makes you feel like you've escaped to paradise. The contemporary decor is both soothing and comforting, and the same feeling is carried throughout the seventy guest rooms and suites. Many rooms even have their own plunge pools. There are three beautiful full-size pools here, too, and while the Tides could easily qualify as a romantic escape, it's also the perfect place to come alone if you want to avoid the crowds and spend some time with yourself. It's romantic without being in-your-face couples-only, and the people I've met here are always happy to include you in their conversations.

For other options about where to stay in Zihuatanejo, start at www.visitmexico.com. This website has a summary of all the major tourist destinations in the area, links to the different hotels, and other tourist information.

▲ *The Tides Resort, Zihuatanejo, Mexico*
© THE TIDES RESORT/CHRISTIAN HORAN

DESTINATION: *New Zealand*

New Zealand is a fantastic place to visit on your own because the people, known as Kiwis, are outrageously friendly and helpful! It doesn't hurt, either, that this is an English-speaking country, which makes it even easier to get around by yourself.

A common complaint is that New Zealand is so far away—and that's true. There's no denying it's going to take you a long flight to get to this little gem of a country, but if you catch a direct flight from the West Coast you can make the trip in about twelve hours. This would be a really good time to trade in those frequent flyer miles and upgrade to first or business class, or at least be sure to get a good seat so you're not trapped, sandwiched into a center seat. (See "THAT'S MY SEAT!" in Chapter Four.)

Since you're flying so far, consider staying in New Zealand as long as you can. This is a tough trip to make in just five days. My first trip there, I stayed for two weeks, which gave me a great opportunity to explore the different parts of the country. Usually when you're traveling through New Zealand you go from one end of the country to the other, which saves time and money because you're not crisscrossing destinations.

There's so much to see and do in New Zealand that it's hard to narrow down your choices, but if you have limited time my favorite TRAVEL THERAPY spots running from south to north are:

- Queenstown: This southern New Zealand resort town has it all, from breathtaking mountain scenery, to fantastic resorts with top-of-the-line dining, spas, and shopping options.
- Christchurch: The Avon River weaves its way through this charming, historic town. Christchurch is full of fun museums and art galleries.
- Milford Sound: People come from all over the world to take a boat ride on Milford Sound, part of the famed Fiordlands. From the waterfalls to the majestic peaks, the scenery here is incredible, making it one of the most beautiful places in New Zealand.
- Auckland: Here you're just a few minutes away from stunning beaches, islands, and hiking trails—and you can get a true taste of Polynesian culture.
- Rotorua: Volcano-country beauty meets adventure junky's paradise—here you can try skydiving to get your thrill on!

New Zealand is the TRAVEL THERAPY for you if you enjoy spending time outdoors. But whether you're into horseback riding, hiking, boating, skiing, or even watching a sheep-shearing demonstration, factor in the time of year you're planning to visit since the seasons are opposite of what we have in the States. Since New Zealand is so far south of the equator, our summers are their winters and vice versa.

Because New Zealand is so spread out, consider planning an independent tour so your stops and transportation are planned ahead of time. If you're all solo traveled out and you're looking for some company at some point during your stay, you can also sign up for some interesting group tours, too.

If you're on a budget, New Zealand is a fantastic place to visit on your own because it has more than three hundred hostels, some of which charge as little as ten dollars a night. Talk about an affordable place to stay! Staying in hostels is also a fun way to meet other travelers who are going it alone and taking advantage of the bargain rates. If this sounds like something you're interested in, check out the Youth Hostels Association of New Zealand (www.yha.co.nz). This comprehensive site has all the information you need to track down the best hostels to fit your itinerary.

If you'd rather stay in a traditional hotel, then the official site of Tourism New Zealand (www.newzealand.com) is the best place to start your search. This site will help you narrow down your hotel choices and map out your itinerary. Wherever you decide to go, make sure you take in some of New Zealand's unique culture. New Zealand's indigenous Maori people bring their own Polynesian artistic style and flavor to the island country, so try to catch a Maori culture exhibit or two. There's a great one in Auckland if you're passing through. Learning about the Maori people will give you a better understanding of the unique cultural mix that makes New Zealand so special.

DESTINATION: *Switzerland*

I love chocolate, cheese, and fondue, so of course I think Switzerland is fabulous. This is an outdoor person's paradise! Every time I visit I discover something new that inspires me. Whether you visit in the dead of winter, when Switzerland turns into a mystical winter wonderland, or the full bloom of summer, when the window boxes on homes are overflowing with flowers, this is a country that always shines.

Clean, safe, and sane Switzerland is an ideal TRAVEL THERAPY destination if you want to travel alone in Europe. Getting around is a piece of cake because the rail service is impeccable. Switzerland is also more affordable than a lot of Europe because it doesn't use the euro; it uses the Swiss franc, so the American dollar holds more value. Probably the hardest thing you're going to encounter is deciding which cities to visit because there are so many worth seeing. As much as I love skiing in the winter, I'm partial to visiting in the spring and summer months when you can enjoy the outdoors and explore the different lake regions without worrying about the freezing temperatures.

My favorite TRAVEL THERAPY Switzerland haunts are:

- Geneva: On the western tip of Switzerland, this tiny city is overflowing with diverse cultures, so you'll find delicious global cuisine and scrumptious chocolates.

- Zurich: This northern city isn't just about banking anymore. It's the place to come if you're looking for sensational shopping and a lively dining scene.

- Basel: Art lovers, don't miss this charming city in northern Switzerland where Switzerland, Germany, and France meet.

- Lucerne: With its cobblestone streets and medieval architecture, you'll be enchanted with all that Lucerne has to offer.

- Lausanne: Situated above Lake Geneva, Lausanne is Switzerland's sexiest city—full of sizzle and fantastic entertainment options.

- Saint Moritz: This is the place to go in southern Switzerland if you're looking for glitz and glam—a holiday resort area known as a favorite escape for the rich and famous.

- Zermatt: Known as a winter playground, Zermatt is also a fantastic summer destination where the Matterhorn rules!

You can easily fall in love with any one of these cities and spend your entire vacation at one location, but if you have the chance, try to visit several places. I always feel inspired and invigorated after visiting Switzerland. The combination of the majestic scenery, friendly people, delicious dining, and outdoor activity options have a way of charming you so you want to visit again and again.

"I have done most of my traveling alone, but it never stays that way for long. I have found that there is beauty everywhere and amazing people to meet in every culture. It's pretty simple, if I haven't been there yet, I want to go there, and when I get there, I know I will leave forever changed in a small, yet profound way. Through travel I have found purpose in my life and discovered my passion for living it fully. Through travel I continue to add a little more to my soul and leave a little of my heart behind everywhere I go."

—TRISHA HARRIS, MILITARY PHOTOGRAPHER, KUWAIT CITY, KUWAIT

LESSON LEARNED
An Old Dog Can Learn New Tricks!

If you're facing those hideous doldrums, where everything seems bland and boring, then a fantastic way to spice up your life is by signing on for a vacation where you can learn something new. Part of reinventing yourself is stretching your wings and seeing how far you can fly outside your usual boundaries. By learning a new craft or trade, you're broadening your horizons and opening yourself up to new possibilities.

If you really want to push yourself, try something you never thought you'd be able to do, or something you've always wanted to try but never found the time. This is your chance to experience an adventure like no other. Of course, it doesn't hurt if you pick a splendid destination to learn this new skill. I like to be inspired by my surroundings and have always believed that the right atmosphere helps promote creativity. So take the plunge. Sign up for a learning vacation. Knowledge is power!

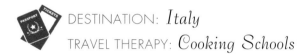

DESTINATION: *Italy*

TRAVEL THERAPY: *Cooking Schools*

I've never been a huge fan of cooking. The microwave is my friend. But after learning some of the tricks of the trade, I found preparing a magnificent meal isn't brain surgery after all. It's actually a great stress-buster to spend some time in the kitchen concentrating on something besides my BlackBerry. The recipe for success when it comes to learning to cook is picking a delicious destination— like Italy.

Right about now you may be thinking, *Wait a minute, I don't even cook!* Don't panic. Even if your idea of putting together a meal means running to the corner restaurant to pick up takeout, there's hope for you. You don't have to be a master chef to enroll in an Italian cooking school. Remember, this TRAVEL THERAPY is all about reinventing who you are and learning new things. Maybe there's a chef hiding somewhere in your soul that you don't even know about. If there's something enticing about the idea of this trip, then trust your gut, grab your apron, and get ready to cook up one fantastic vacation.

When it comes to deciding what school to enroll in, start by picking the part of Italy you'd like to visit and then narrowing it down from there. The Italian Government Tourist Board has put together a great website at www.italiantourism.com that will help you learn about the different areas of Italy. Once you're done there, head over to the Italian Language and Culture Schools in Italy website (www.it-schools.com) to find your school. Just click on the part of the country you want to visit and schools in that area will pop up. Here are some top Travel Therapy recommendations:

- The Italian Cookery Course: www.italiancookerycourse.com
- Villa Giona: www.villagiona.it
- Regaleali: www.absoluteitalia.com

- Cucina con Vista: www.cucinaconvista.it
- Villa San Michele: www.villasanmichele .com

Another thing to consider is the kind of accommodations you're looking for. Each cooking school offers something different— from simple to elaborate digs where you can stay in anything from an old monastery to a place with a dormlike setting. Also decide how long you want your cooking vacation to be. In the schools mentioned above, you can find those that only last a few days or those that run for several weeks. Be sure to consider all the factors before you sign up and grab your chef's hat.

DESTINATION: *Montana*

TRAVEL THERAPY: *Dude Ranches*

The first time I visited Montana I was moving there for a new job. I was coming from California and wasn't quite prepared for the country way of life. I stopped at a bar for a cold drink and got sawdust stuck in my sandals. A few minutes later, I felt something tug around my ankles and turned around to find out that it was a lasso with a laughing cowboy attached to the other end. I swear, you can't make up this kind of story! Welcome to Montana.

Despite the initial shock, it was easy to fall in love with Montana's scenery and warm-hearted people. But to really understand the country life, you have to head to a dude ranch. This is one of my favorite Travel Therapy destinations for city slickers because of the noticeable transformation you go through after spending just a short time on a ranch. Signing up to do something that's not part of your normal reality is the perfect way to shake things up a bit and open your eyes to a new way of life.

If you want to push yourself, head to a dude ranch where part of your stay means actually doing some ranch work. That's right,

actual ranch work where you get up at the crack of dawn and work until the sun goes down. Think you can take it? Let's see. It's one thing to want to hang out at a pretty ranch and sip some coffee; it's another thing entirely to get up at five in the morning to make that coffee.

So what exactly do you do on a dude ranch? That depends on the kind of ranch you pick, but you can be assured that you'll do some riding and go on a cattle or horse drive. A lot of ranches in Montana also throw in some fishing. The price for a dude ranch vacation varies, so you'll want to do some research before you decide.

The Dude Ranchers' Association website is a cool spot to check out (www.duderanch.org). The Dude Ranchers' Association was formed back in 1926. These folks take their jobs very seriously, and not just anyone can join. Ranchers have to apply and go through a tough two-year inspection process, so you know when you're checking out ranches on this site that you're getting the best of the best.

A couple that ranked high on the list for Montana include Dryhead Ranch (www.dryheadranch.com) and Sweet Grass Ranch (www.sweetgrassranch.com).

If you like the idea of a dude ranch vacation, but you're not quite ready to get your hands *that* dirty, don't worry. Montana doesn't disappoint. The Big Sky Country also boasts luxurious dude ranches. A top award-winner is the Triple Creek Ranch (www.triplecreekranch.com). At this showstopper you don't have to lift a finger unless you want a sip of champagne. This adult-only retreat caters to people looking to lasso the finer things in life. Giddyap!

DESTINATION: *France*

TRAVEL THERAPY: *Chocolate Making*

Chocolate lovers rejoice, because this is one sweet Travel Therapy idea. If your mouth is already watering at the thought of being surrounded by dark, lush chocolate, then this is the trip for you. Some of best chocolate makers in the world can be found in the area around Lyon, France, in the famed Rhone-Alpes region. This is where you'll find Valrhona (www.valrhona.com), an award-winning chocolate company that's willing to share its delicious secrets and teach you all the chocolate-making tricks of the trade. Can you think of a better reason for going to school?

Valrhona's Ecole du Grand Chocolat is just outside of Lyon and holds its classes at the

◀ *Triple Creek Ranch, Darby, Montana*
© TRIPLE CREEK RANCH

company's headquarters in Tain l'Hermitage. If the closest you've ever come to working with chocolate is peeling off a candy wrapper, don't worry, there are several beginner classes you can take. In one course you learn how to make chocolate cookies, mousse, and cakes; in another you get right to the heart of the matter and learn how to make truffles and chocolate-filled candies. Another plus, all classes are offered in both French and English.

Another great website to check out for chocolate-making classes is Ecole Chocolat (www.ecolechocolat.com), where you can find all kinds of chocolate classes and some interesting history about the chocolate-making progress. What makes this TRAVEL THERAPY even more irresistible is the fact that these special chocolate classes are taught in one of the most beautiful areas of France. If you want to learn more about the Rhone-Alpes region, the tourism office has a nifty little website, www.rhonealpes-tourism .co.uk, which is regularly updated with new information about the latest travel trends and places to stay in the area.

AUTHOR'S PICK

DESTINATION: *South Africa*

When I was in high school, I had a friend who'd traveled to South Africa several times, and I was fascinated by her stories about the country. I desperately wanted to go, and so I tucked it away in the back of my mind as a place I'd someday make it to. It took years to find the time and money, but South Africa was worth the wait.

As a country, South Africa offers so many different vacation experiences that it's hard to nail down where to start. A good plan is to at least include visits to Johannesburg, Cape Town, and Kruger National Park. Before my trip, some South Africans I know advised me to get out of Johannesburg as quickly as possible and see the other parts of the country, but there were things in Johannesburg that I wanted to see. The Apartheid Museum (www .apartheidmuseum.org) was top on my list.

You'll want to plan at least three hours for your visit. The museum opened its doors in 2001 and walks you through the history of South Africa under apartheid. The displays are haunting, and the photographs and videos can be hard to take in, but you leave the museum with a better understanding of

the struggle of South Africa. A visit to the museum also helps you appreciate the challenges this country and its people have been through, so when you're touring different parts of South Africa, you have a sense of history and perspective about the past. Other favorite stops in Johannesburg include:

- Soweto: This is the largest township in South Africa and an excellent place to try some authentic South African food.

- Cradle of Humankind Tour: Take a step back in time and see fossilized remains that date back two to three million years.

- Hector Pieterson Memorial and Museum: This museum is a moving tribute to Hector Pieterson and his fellow students, who were gunned down and killed in a 1976 student protest.

It's no secret that Johannesburg is a city that battles crime issues, so it's important that you pick a safe place to stay in a part of the city you'll feel comfortable getting around in. Top on the list, if money isn't an issue,

▲ *View of Cape Town, South Africa, from the Ellerman House*
© KAREN SCHALER

is the Saxon Boutique Hotel & Spa (www
.saxon.co.za), one of the most luxurious hotels in all of South Africa. This award-winning
exclusive boutique property has twenty-four
impressive suites and is a celebrity favorite.
After he was released from prison, Nelson
Mandela stayed here while he worked on his
book *Long Walk to Freedom*.

Insider tip: If you want to see where Mr.
Mandela wrote his book, you don't need to
stay in the pricey Nelson Mandela Suite. The
hotel staff says he actually wrote the book in
what has now been converted into the hotel's
business center.

Another popular choice for a first-class
experience is the Westcliff (www.westcliff
.co.za). This world-class hotel is perched high
on a cliff in the northwestern suburbs overlooking the city. Even if you don't stay here,
it is definitely worth having breakfast on the
balcony so you can take in the amazing view.

After taking in all the sites in Johannesburg, head to Cape Town, where you'll find
one of the most gorgeous and picturesque
destinations in South Africa. I found two
amazing boutique properties in Cape Town
that quickly became personal TRAVEL THERAPY
favorites. You can't go wrong staying at either
the Ellerman House (www.ellermanhouse
.com) or the Ezard House (www.ezardhouse
.com). Both are exquisite. If you're looking to
splurge, the Ellerman House has an amazing
private villa right next to the main house that
will take your breath away. Other top choices

include a traditional favorite called Mount
Nelson Hotel (www.mountnelson.co.za),
the Hout Bay Manor (www.houtbaymanor
.co.za), the Vineyard Hotel & Spa (www
.vineyard.co.za), and the funky Daddy Long
Legs Hotel (www.daddylonglegs.co.za).

You'll need at least four days in Cape
Town if you want to even begin to scratch the
surface of what this city has to offer. While
you're exploring don't miss seeing:

- Table Mountain: At this world famous site,
  you can take a cable car to the top of the
  mountain for the most fantastic panoramic
  view of Cape Town.
- Cape of Good Hope: On the tip of the
  Cape Peninsula, this is the perfect place for
  a picnic or scenic drive.
- Robben Island: This is the island where
  Nelson Mandela spent most of his twenty-
  seven years behind bars. The tour includes
  seeing the tiny cell where Mandela lived.
- Constantia Wine Route: A wine
  connoisseur's delight that takes you to some
  of the oldest and most respected wineries in
  South Africa.

Of all the places in South Africa, Kruger
National Park is probably the most well-
known because of its safaris. Some people
fly directly into the park and never experience the other areas of South Africa, but
they don't realize how much they're missing.
(We'll have more on Kruger National Park
coming up in Chapter Ten on page 235.)

For help in planning your South Africa
adventure, a great resource is the website run
by South Africa Tourism at www.southafrica

.net. You can spend hours on this site because there is so much information to go through, but it will give you a solid feel for what this country has to offer so you can make the most of your stay.

After visiting a country like South Africa, where you see such distinct lines between luxury and poverty, you'll be left with a new appreciation for all that you have in the United States. A visit to South Africa opens your eyes and your heart. You go home appreciating the freedom we too often take for granted. South Africa's history and struggles will also remind you that anything is possible if you stay true to what you believe in and never give up the fight.

> *"Travel teaches you tolerance and acceptance of other people and their differences and way of life. It's hard to accept and embrace something you don't understand and traveling rewards you with that knowledge. Stepping out of your comfort zone and into the ways of others opens your eyes and your heart and you're able to meet some wonderful people and make lifelong friends as well."*
>
> —JODY DIAMOND, PRESIDENT DIAMOND PUBLIC RELATIONS, MIAMI, FLORIDA

Reinvent Vacation Checklist

CHOOSE TRIPS WHERE YOU CAN:

- Grow personally
- Learn new things
- Experience a new culture
- Explore a new place
- Try different cuisine
- Challenge your imagination
- Learn a different language
- Open your eyes and your heart

"The journey not the arrival matters."

—T. S. ELIOT

Chapter 10

Just Do It!

*I*f you're looking for a shot of adrenaline or a kick in the butt to finally go after your dreams, this is the TRAVEL THERAPY chapter for you. Whether you've just retired or changed jobs, or desperately want to change some aspect of your life, the mantra you need to memorize is "Just Do It!" What are you waiting for?

Once you've wrapped your mind around the idea that you're ready to take some time for yourself and sign up for a once-in-a-lifetime vacation, there's no reason to hesitate. The clock is ticking. Your destiny is waiting for you!

The following TRAVEL THERAPY destinations have one thing in common. They all require a serious time commitment. You're going to have to clear your calendar and your mind and let the journey be part of your adventure.

Here are the Just Do It! options:

- Finesse the Greens—Golf Vacations
- Hit the Road—Driving Destinations
- Check Out, Indefinitely—Long-term Trips

Which trip is right for you? Take the TRAVEL THERAPY quiz and you're one step closer to making your dream vacation come true.

◀ *Highway 1, Central Coast, California*
© CALIFORNIA TRAVEL & TOURISM COMMISSION

TRAVEL THERAPY QUIZ

1. You want a vacation where you can:

   a. Get some exercise

   b. Drive and see different destinations

   c. Travel all over the world

2. You enjoy driving:

   a. When it involves a golf club

   b. When there are great things to see

   c. Never

3. Would you like to spend several months on a boat?

   a. Not so much—you'd rather be on land

   b. Nope—the car is where it's at

   c. Sounds great, sign me up!

4. A golf vacation sounds:

   a. Amazing

   b. So-so

   c. Nah, not for me

5. You're prepared to travel:

   a. Somewhere warm

   b. For several weeks

   c. For several months

6. When you are traveling, you must have:

   a. Golf clubs

   b. Road maps

   c. A great camera

7. When you hear "green" you think:

   a. Color of a golf course

   b. Green means drive

   c. The amount you'll shell out for your trip

8. The idea of an around-the-world trip has you asking:

   a. Is there golf involved?

   b. Will I be able to drive around?

   c. Where do I sign up?

9. You're ready for:

   a. A golf trip

   b. A driving vacation

   c. An around-the-world tour

10. You would rather be:

    a. Golfing

    b. Driving

    c. Flying or cruising

TRAVEL THERAPY DIAGNOSIS

If you picked mostly "A" answers, then you'll want to dust off your golf clubs and head for a long-term golf vacation where you'll have plenty of time to hit the greens. If "B" is your answer of choice, then get ready to eat up some serious miles because it's time for a road-trip adventure where you're in charge of where you go and how you get there. If "C" is the answer that keeps coming up, then you're ready to splurge and go all out and take that once-in-a-lifetime vacation you've always dreamed about. No matter what you pick, don't let anything get in your way of going on this journey. Just Do It!

DESTINATIONS TO AVOID:

- Short-term trip destinations
- Boring and uninspired destinations
- Places where you aren't challenged
- Places where you can't learn new things
- Places where you don't love what you're doing
- Anyplace where you wish you were somewhere else
- Been there, done that destinations

"Travel is therapy, or at least it can be for those who are willing to let go of rigid schedules and go with the flow as it unfolds. For those who are searching for something more in their lives, the key is to get lost, to give yourself permission to explore new territory, to take constructive risks, and most of all, to surrender to novel experiences that get your attention in ways that nothing else could touch."

—JEFFREY A. KOTTLER, PhD, PROFESSOR, DEPARTMENT OF COUNSELING, CALIFORNIA STATE UNIVERSITY, FULLERTON

FINESSE THE GREENS
Golf Vacations

How many times have you tried to sneak in a game of golf on the weekend only to feel guilty afterward because half your day was spent on the course? Part of the beauty of signing up for a real honest-to-goodness golf vacation is that your golf guilt goes right out the window. By taking a golf-themed trip, you're actually giving yourself permission to enjoy what you love and to spend as much time on the course as daylight allows.

Whether you can take a week or a month, the idea behind this TRAVEL THERAPY trip is to pick a place to play where there are enough options to keep you challenged. If you always buy those glossy golf calendars and wish you could play one of those amazing courses featured in the photographs, now is your chance. The following three golf destinations highlight some of the top-rated courses in the world, including some of the most photographed golf holes. So grab your clubs and get your A-game ready for a first-class golf adventure.

 DESTINATION: *Scotland*

It almost seems cliché to talk about golf and Scotland in the same breath. Scotland is known as the golf capital of the world; and while it's one thing to have that reputation, it's another to actually live up to it. But Scotland does just that.

Scotland is called the "Home of Golf" because this is where golf was born more than six hundred years ago. Today, the country has more than 550 golf courses! In Scotland, you can play year-round, but it can get a little damp and chilly in the winter, which is why the most popular playing months are between April and September. For this golf destination you need to book ahead to be sure you can get on the course of your dreams (and everyone else's), including St. Andrews (www.standrews.org.uk). St. Andrews is one of the most popular courses in the country, with more than forty thousand rounds of golf played there annually. Getting a tee-time at The Old Course is like winning the lottery. Actually, there is a lottery for some of the spots, so if you can't get a tee-time on your first try, check out the lottery system.

To help you map out your play, Scotland's National Tourism Organization has set up a fantastic website at www.visitscotland.com. There's a special golf link that's packed with information about booking the different courses, places to stay, golf etiquette, and more. Here you'll also find some great insider information, like the fact that throughout the country you can play golf until ten at night. That's right, ten at *night*. In the summer, through September, it gets light in Scotland at around five in the morning and stays light until ten in the evening so you have some great extra golf hours.

There are actually six different golf regions in Scotland. If you have the time, hitting each one would make for an excellent vacation. If you don't, then figure out the places you want to play most and save the rest for your next trip. Trust me, there will be a next trip because after you visit Scotland once you'll be hooked.

Also be sure to look into special package deals and golf passes where you can save some big bucks. Many of the hotels in the area also offer fabulous "stay and play" golf vacations, so as long as you give yourself plenty of lead time, you should be able to come up with some sensational and affordable options. Some top Travel Therapy Scotland courses include:

- Royal Troon Golf Club: www.royaltroon.co.uk
- Prestwick Golf Club: www.prestwickgc.co.uk
- The Machrie Hotel and Golf Links: www.machrie.com
- Loch Lomond Golf Club: www.lochlomond.com
- The Westin Turnberry Resort: www.turnberry.co.uk
- Carnoustie Golf Links: www.carnoustiegolflinks.co.uk

 DESTINATION: *Riviera Maya, Mexico*

Hola, Mexico golf! Mexico is a hole-in-one destination where golf is concerned, with some spectacular new world-class courses. Better known for its sugar sand beaches and mouthwatering margaritas, the scenic Riviera Maya area of Mexico has also successfully added luxury golf to its outstanding features. A fantastic Travel Therapy option for golfers is to start your trip just outside of Cancun and make the trek down to Tulum, playing different golf courses along the way. Part of the magic in this trip is mixing inspiring golf with some sensational sightseeing. You can alternate hitting the greens and relaxing on the beach and make this one golf vacation you'll never forget.

When it comes to the top courses along the Riviera Maya, two new award-winning Greg Norman designed courses are where it's at. El Camaleón (www.mayakobagolf.com) is only about thirty-five miles south of Cancun, and it's Norman's first course in Mexico. When you're playing this challenging beauty, you'll never get bored because one minute you're hitting into the jungle and the next you might be shooting toward the ocean. El Camaleón is designed to blend in with the local environment so you'll find yourself weaving in and out of mangroves. Some holes even have you playing right next to huge ancient *cenotes* (caves), so you'll want to watch your step and have your camera ready!

Another top pick in the area is Playa Mujeres Golf Club (www.troongolf.com). Just five miles outside of Cancun, this challenging course features tight fairways and tricky trade winds. This course has its own driving range, two putting greens, and a short game practice area. A bonus is that this course welcomes female golfers with open arms. Playa Mujeres, which literally means "Women's Beach", is the first course in Latin America that's certified as "women friendly" by the Executive Women's Golf Association (EWGA). Bravo!

For more on the different golf courses along the Riviera Maya and unique "stay and play" golf package options, check out the Mexico Tourism Board's site at www.visit mexico.com.

"Retirement means a big change in one's life. When my husband retired without a hobby or sport to fall back on, we decided on a complete change of lifestyle. We wanted to travel. We drove to Mexico and bought a home in a small village where every day was a challenge while we learned to cope with a new environment, a new language, and new people. Those were the busiest and happiest days of our lives."

—PAT CRANE, RETIRED, BELLINGHAM, WASHINGTON

DESTINATION: *Scottsdale/Phoenix, Arizona*

When the weather turns wet, soggy, and cold, golf fans from all over the world flock to Arizona by the thousands to take advantage of the year-round sunshine and amazing golf courses. While you'll find great golf opportunities all around the state, the Scottsdale/Phoenix area is the true superstar when it comes to a first-class golf experience.

While this is an ideal TRAVEL THERAPY destination for a quick weekend golf fix, you'll want to stay at least several weeks, to try out as many courses as possible, if you're going for the ultimate experience. The Scottsdale/

Phoenix area has more than two hundred golf courses to choose from. Many of the courses were designed by golf legends, so whatever kind of play you're looking for, chances are you can find it in the Valley of the Sun.

A smart option for an Arizona golf vacation is to rent a fully furnished vacation rental. Hotels in the area can get pretty spendy during the popular winter months, but there are always several hundred homes and condo

▲ *Troon North Golf Club, Monument Course Hole 15, Scottsdale, Arizona*
© TROON GOLF

rentals available where everything's included. Vacation rentals are big business in Arizona, so you shouldn't have any problems finding something at a great price in the specific area you're looking for.

For helping with hunting down the best deals, two of the best websites are www.vacationrentals.com and www.vacationhomerental.com. Both sites offer photographs of the rentals, reviews from other guests, and all kinds of insider information about the area. Most rentals are by month, but even if you only need a place for two weeks, check out the prices because it could still be cheaper than what you'd pay at a local hotel.

With so many golf courses to choose from, you shouldn't have a problem getting tee-times whenever you want to golf, but it's still smart to reserve ahead for the most popular courses. You'll also want to check out the official Scottsdale and Phoenix websites (www.scottsdalecvb.com and www.visitphoenix.com) because both have extensive golf listings and give you up-to-date information about specials and different "stay and play" packages at the top resorts.

Besides the impeccable weather, the other draw of a golf vacation in Scottsdale/Phoenix is the area itself. There is so much to do after you finish your eighteen holes—top restaurants, spas, shopping, and entertainment—that you'll want to be sure to plan some time off the course just to explore this evolving desert community.

HIT THE ROAD
Driving Destinations

If the idea of a long, extended vacation sounds perfect as long as you don't have to get on a plane, then this is the TRAVEL THERAPY option for you! There are so many incredible driving destinations around the world that it's hard to narrow down three top picks. But each of the following options go above and beyond your typical road trip.

The idea behind a driving destination is to take control of your journey and go exactly where you want to go at your own pace. A huge plus when it comes to a driving vacation is that you get to avoid all the hassles at the airport. If you're renting a vehicle, be sure you have the proper insurance, and that you pick a ride that fits your plan. A convertible is an awesome choice if you're riding along the coast, but if you plan to go off the beaten path then you might want to consider a four-wheel drive. How much luggage you're hauling with you will also determine how much space you need. Also, remember to buckle up!

While a driving vacation can help you avoid the annoyance of air travel, remember that driving for hours in a car can get claustrophobic if you don't plan interesting places to get out and stretch your legs. When you're deciding on your budget, be sure to consider fuel prices in the towns you'll be traveling through. A fantastic resource to help you figure out your finances is AAA's Fuel Cost Calculator (www.fuelcostcalculator.com). This cool website has you put in where you're going and the kind of vehicle you're driving and then gives an idea of exactly how far you're traveling and what it will cost in fuel.

Hitting the open road with a map and a mission, where you don't have to worry about how long you're gone, is invigorating. On this TRAVEL THERAPY journey, the road you're traveling down is literally the road you've chosen. Don't be afraid to venture off your planned itinerary if something you see sparks your interest. That's the beauty of a driving destination. At any moment, depending on where you're driving, you can change your course and start a whole new journey. The possibilities are endless.

 DESTINATION: *California Coast*

Driving along the California coast is the ultimate feeling of freedom. Nothing can compare to the experience of zipping around a twisting corner and discovering a stunning stretch of beach or a breathtaking strip of shoreline that seems to stretch on forever. The reason you should drive on Highway 1 is because of the sensational scenery, so have your camera ready. Be careful where you stop, though, because it's a very narrow stretch of highway and pulling over to park can be dangerous if you don't pick the right place.

No matter how many times you take this drive, you will always discover something new. If you're in a hurry and trying to get from one end of the state to the other, the coastal route is obviously not the way to go. But if you have time on your hands, and your goal is to explore this unique part of California, you won't find a better road trip along the West Coast than the Pacific Coast Highway.

A great place to start your coastal crusade is in Santa Cruz, California. From there you can just follow the coast all the way down to San Diego. In perfect driving conditions it takes between eight and nine hours to travel between San Francisco and Los Angeles on Highway 1, but that's without stopping. So if you factor in making stops along the way, you'll want to plan at least a week to make this trip. You don't want your relaxing vacation to be all about just zooming down the highway. You want to make sure you have the time to stop and experience the different communities and sightseeing opportunities along the way.

Deciding where to stop is tough, but the California Travel & Tourism Commission has some great suggestions on its website at www.visitcalifornia.com. Not only are there links to the different communities along the coast, but you can also map out your route and get rough estimates of how long it will take to travel between point A and B.

Some favorite TRAVEL THERAPY stops to make include:

- Hearst Castle: The palatial architecture alone makes Hearst Castle worth the trip. With more than one hundred and sixty rooms, the castle was donated by the Hearst family to the state, and it's now open for tours.
- 17-mile Drive: Dare to dream when you travel this route through the famed golf community of Pebble Beach where you'll find multi-million dollar mansions lining the ocean.
- Carmel-by-the-Sea: This world-class beach destination is consistently ranked top in the country for its beauty and charm.

- Big Sur: Known for being a great escape and a romantic destination, Big Sur delivers in a big way.
- Cambria: A beautiful coastal community where you can find hiking and biking trails along with great surfing.
- Newport Beach: From bohemian to swanky, Newport Beach has it all—including some sensational surfing.
- Laguna Beach: This artsy, creative community is always worth a stop to see what kinds of treasures you can uncover.

Before you set out on your California journey, check the road conditions. There are some areas of Highway 1, like Devil's Slide, that are prone to rock slides, which can end up shutting down the highway. It's also a good idea to plan a few places where you want to stay along the route and get reservations ahead of time. If you roll into a popular stop like Big Sur late in the afternoon, there's a good chance some of the best deals will have already been snatched up. Be sure to bring a good map, some snacks, binoculars, and your camera, and get ready for a California adventure like no other.

"I decided to leave my traditional job and take a job with a major airline so I could fly for free and see as much of the world as possible. Now I'm able to get away for all sorts of adventures. Traveling for free is a great reason to get up and go to work!"

—BEVA SMITH, AIRLINE EMPLOYEE, SCOTTSDALE, ARIZONA

 DESTINATION: *The Big Island, Hawaii*

When a friend and I lived on the Big Island of Hawaii one summer, we decided that we needed to plan a trip all the way around the island. We had heard it was the perfect way to check out our new "home," and it turned out to be one of the most beautiful coastal trips I've ever taken. We asked some locals about the best places to stop, and within no time had a long list of suggestions. Hawaiians call driving around to see what you can see *ho-loholo*. The concept is a popular one, making this an excellent choice for a TRAVEL THERAPY driving destination.

The Big Island is the youngest of the Hawaiian Islands, and it's also the largest with almost three hundred miles of coastline. Covering more than four thousand square miles, this island is great to drive around because there are so many different ecological areas to discover and appreciate. From the gorgeous beaches at sea level to the always-impressive Kilauea Volcano, Hawaii will keep you guessing. Most of the roads are just two

▲ *Oceanside Drive, Punta, The Big Island, Hawaii*
© BIG ISLAND VISITORS BUREAU

lanes, so you have to stay alert. If you're driving with someone else, take turns so you both can take in the sights and relax.

While it's possible to drive around the island in one day, it's much more rewarding to take your time and stay a few nights in the different communities along the coast. By getting off the road and venturing into the different towns, you gain a better appreciation for what makes this island so memorable. This is another trip where you want to be sure to have your camera ready because the scenery is postcard perfect and there's usually an amazing photo opportunity around every corner.

Some Travel Therapy favorite spots to stop and explore along your drive around the island include:

- Akaka Falls State Park: If you like waterfalls, this is the place you want to go.
- Waipio Valley Lookout: Here you'll get a great view of the Waipio ("Curved Water")

Valley.

- World Botanical Gardens: A great place to get out and stretch your legs and take in some tropical scenery.
- Kealakekua Bay: This Marine Life Conservation District is ideal for snorkeling and scuba diving.
- Holualoa: An artists' community where you can find all kinds of things you'll want to take home.

For help with planning your Hawaii road trip, go directly to the Big Island Visitors Bureau website at www.bigisland.org. You'll find some great scenic videos that can give you a feel for what you can experience on the island. The website also has some smart suggestions on how to plan your trip, including places you'll want to see and where you'll want to stay and eat. There's even a link for a volcano update—it's not a bad idea to know how active it is before you start your tour around the island.

 DESTINATION: *New England*

My favorite time to drive in New England is when the summer slips into fall and the landscape explodes in brilliant bursts of autumn foliage. While traveling through the New England states is wonderful any time of year, making the trip during the fall harvest season is stunning. If you've never made the drive before and can't decide where to begin, a great place to start is in New Hampshire, where there are more than a dozen official scenic drives designated to help you find your way. This New England state is also a manageable size, allowing you to explore all four corners of this state in a short time.

New Hampshire is covered with maple, elm, oak, beech, pine, and fir trees, and peak

leaf-peeping season usually hits between September and October. Since the best hotels and bed-and-breakfasts can fill up fast, be sure to book your favorite choices ahead of time so you can be sure to get the rooms you want.

For help with exactly where to go, how to find the best places to stay, or specific details about fall foliage routes try the official website for the New Hampshire division of travel and tourism at www.visitnh.gov. After you've checked out the site and have mapped out a general plan of action, be sure to give yourself enough time to travel so that you can really appreciate the area during this stunning time of year.

The different scenery you'll see in New Hampshire reaches out and pulls you in. No matter how tired or stressed you're feeling, a trip where you're surrounded by blazes of orange, yellow, and red can give you the energy boost you need. Try to look for places to drive that most people aren't as likely to travel. Some of the best discoveries I've ever made have happened when I turned off the road I was supposed to be on and found myself surrounded by spectacular vistas with no one else in sight.

▲ *Upper Oxbow Road in New Hampshire*
© DALE W. LARY

CHECK OUT, INDEFINITELY
Long-term Trips

If you have unlimited time on your hands and you're craving a once-in-a-lifetime adventure that will have you exploring all four corners of the world, then this is the TRAVEL THERAPY option for you.

The idea behind an around-the-world trip is to sign up for a vacation where you pay up front and let someone else handle the planning and logistics. This way you have all the benefits of global travel without any of the headaches.

Around-the-world tours vary from trips where you fly commercial airlines to various places around the globe to ultra-exclusive world tours where you fly in private jets or travel by a luxury cruise ship.

No matter how you decide to travel, this is not the trip to take if you only have a few weeks. It's no fun spending half of your vacation traveling to your destination only to turn around and come home a few days later. If you're going to take this kind of trip then you really need to commit to the time it takes to do it right.

This TRAVEL THERAPY journey is all about discovering places in the world you've only dreamed about. Maybe you've talked about doing a trip like this but have always made excuses that you didn't have the time or money. If there's a trip out there that you've always wanted to do, then you need to follow the mantra that embodies the spirit of this chapter and Just Do It!

"I think the concept that has been made very clear to me through my travel around the world is how much we, as Americans, take for granted and how much simpler the rest of the world lives. I found many of the people who are very poor still live cleanly and are happy. They have fewer worries than we do and they protect their heritage and traditions because that is what is most valuable to them. Travel has humbled me."

—KAREN STARK, ARTIST, WASHOUGAL, WASHINGTON

DESTINATION: *Australia*

Opals, the outback, outrageous diving, and snorkeling—Australia has all that and much more. As a destination, Australia is much larger than most people think. It's actually the sixth largest country in the world, so when you consider that it's roughly the size of the United States, it starts to make sense why you need at least two weeks to visit. Even a direct flight from the West Coast will take you twelve hours, so if you're going to invest the flying time, you might as well make sure you have enough time on the ground to experience this extraordinary country without rushing around.

The first time I visited Australia I stayed for ten days and I left feeling like there was so much more I needed to see. When I made a list of all the places I'd missed, I couldn't help but wonder what I'd actually done. I had crisscrossed the country and covered a lot of ground, including the Australian outback, the Great Barrier Reef, and various cities and beaches in between, but I still had a long list of things I'd missed. I didn't get a chance to visit Melbourne or Wellington, two top-rated cities, and I would have liked to have spent more time exploring Sydney. Of course, you can't see everything in just two weeks—and besides, it gives you a good excuse to go back.

One of the reasons Australia is such an exciting destination is because it's halfway around the globe from the United States, and there are so many things that are completely different from home. You truly feel as if you're on an adventure. At one moment you might be snorkeling or diving near a place where great white sharks live and the next you might be trekking through the outback, climbing Ayers Rock. It's wild and wonderful all rolled into one fascinating country.

For your journey to the "Land Down Under," check out the official site for Australian Travel and Tourism (www.australia.com), which is packed with fantastic insider information on the best places to visit and explore. Tourism Australia (www.tourism.australia.com) is another helpful website that includes all the major players in Australia's tourism industry. Here you can research travel trends and the history of Australia tourism to give you a better feel for the country you're visiting.

Before you go, try on a few fun Aussie words like *g'day* (good day), *bonza* (great), and *mate* (friend) and get comfortable using them. That way you'll be a hit with the friendly locals who love to share their fabulous part of the world with visitors from other countries.

HASTA LA VISTA! *Tips for Long-term Trips*

If you're headed off on an adventure that's going to keep you away from home for more than the usual one-week trip, then you need to plan ahead. By following these simple Travel Therapy tips you can come home rested and relaxed and stay that way!

· Make sure all bills are paid in advance so you don't have late fees.

· Have the post office hold your mail.

· Unplug all unnecessary appliances.

· Have someone maintain your yard if needed.

· Have someone water your plants and check on your place.

· Give someone a set of keys in case there's an emergency.

· Leave your itinerary and passport information with friends or family.

· Have enough prescriptions filled to last your entire trip.

· Bring an extra copy of your prescriptions with you.

· Bring extra cash, just in case.

· Pack only what's needed, then take a fourth of what you've packed out.

 DESTINATION: *Around-The-World Cruising*

Around-the-world cruises are growing in popularity as savvy travelers are demanding more exotic global vacation options. What you need for these special TRAVEL THERAPY trips is time and money—and lots of both! There are luxury world cruises that can last more than one hundred days. Talk about your ultimate TRAVEL THERAPY escape!

The Regent Seven Seas Cruises made history in early 2009 by offering the first two world cruise itineraries in the same year. The two ships, the Seven Seas Voyager and the Seven Seas Mariner, each hold only seven hundred guests, to keep the cruising experience more intimate. The rooms are generous-size suites with private balconies, so it's first-class all the way. The Seven Seas Voyager will hit global hot spots like Australia, Shanghai, Dubai, and Istanbul, and stops for the Seven Seas Mariner include

Buenos Aires, Santiago, Sydney, Singapore, and Hong Kong.

Here's a list of some other top TRAVEL THERAPY picks if you're considering cruising around the world:

- Holland America Line: www.hollandamerica.com
- Cunard: www.cunard.com
- Crystal Cruises: www.crystalcruises.com
- Silversea: www.silversea.com

A great resource to scout out world cruises is www.cruising.org. Just be sure, before you sign up for one of these lengthy cruises, that you actually *like* cruising. If you've never been on a cruise ship before, you should try signing up for a shorter two-week trip just to make sure you don't get seasick or claustrophobic. Three to four months is a long time to spend on a ship, no matter how posh and perfect it is, so make sure you have your sea legs before you shell out the big bucks for a world-wide trip.

▲ *Regent Seven Seas Voyager near Nice, France*
© REGENT SEVEN SEAS CRUISES

DESTINATION: *Around-The-World Flying*

If you love the idea of circling the globe but you don't want to be confined to a ship, there are several top-rated around-the-world tour options where you either fly commercial or in a private jet to get to your different destinations.

TCS Expeditions (www.tcs-expeditions .com) is a great resource for researching long-term global trips. One of the most exclusive options is the twenty-five day Around the World Classic, where you travel by private jet to each destination, which cuts down on the time you would waste at airports waiting for commercial flights. TCS has been offering around-the-world travel by private jet since 1995, and the company says plans for the future include adding even more destinations and options for discriminating travelers. Some of the unique destinations on the Around the World Classic trip have included Machu Picchu, Easter Island, Samoa, Papua New Guinea, and Cambodia.

Other top tour companies offering similar around-the-world travel include Starquest Expeditions (www.starquest expeditions.com) and Abercrombie & Kent (www.abercrombiekent.com).

Depending on what you're looking for, most of these world-tour trips span several weeks to several months and can cost anywhere from $20,000 to over $100,000 per person. This is a huge time and financial investment, so you want to make sure you pick the tour company that's right for you. Do your research and try to find people who have taken similar trips and ask them what they liked and what they would have done differently.

This is your once-in-a-lifetime chance for a travel experience like no other. By traveling around the world, you're able to soak up different cultural experiences, gaining experiences and knowledge that will fuel you forward in every aspect of your life. You will not come home the same person. You will be better for what you've seen, the people you have met, and the friends you've made along the way. It's worth the investment in more ways than one.

Once you find the trip you want, make a commitment to yourself about when it might be realistic to make this happen. It may require putting aside some money every month or deciding to do the trip when you're between jobs, or after you retire. But do yourself a favor and write down your goal—and don't make it five or ten years out. You deserve this. Remember, this is all about doing something that will change your life, so don't hesitate. Just Do It!

AUTHOR'S PICK

DESTINATION: *Safari, Kruger National Park, South Africa*

A safari trip had been on my "to-do" list since I was a teenager, but it would take decades before I could finally clear two weeks in my hectic schedule to make the trip happen. In the first ten years of my professional career, I never had more than five days off at a time, so the safari dream was put on hold indefinitely. It wasn't until I came to a personal and professional crossroads that I was able to finally realize my dream in 2008. I had just returned from reporting in Afghanistan and realized how precious and short life is. I didn't want to wait any longer, so I quit my full-time job, bought my ticket, and never looked back.

Before taking the trip, I talked to at least two-dozen people who had piles of advice on where to go for the best animal sightings and safari experience. Over and over again there was one place that kept coming up: the Kruger National Park in South Africa.

I had always heard that safaris were outrageously expensive and might run me as much as $3,000 a night. Since that was way out of my price range I kept looking for more affordable options. It turns out you can actually stay in Kruger for around $75 dollars a night if you pick one of the park's rest camps, like Skukuza (www.krugerpark.co.za), where you can stay in a tent or a simple bungalow. You can also save bucks by doing your own self-guided driving safari, where you can just

▲ *A Lion Resting in South Africa's Kruger National Park*
© KAREN SCHALER

rent a 4x4 and drive yourself around in the park seeing what you can see. Also, if you visit during the off-season, between May and August, the weather is much cooler and it's actually a better time to see more wildlife.

Still, if you want a truly authentic African safari experience, your best choice is to get away from the crowds and stay on a private game reserve or a private concession. The cost can skyrocket, but with a little work you can still find some affordable options. The private reserves and concessions aren't fenced-in properties, so you're living in the wild when staying at these camps. You're constantly surrounded by animals. It's not unusual to look out your bedroom window and see a giraffe or zebra stroll by. These camps are also smaller, usually allowing less than twelve people, giving you a much more intimate experience. Most are all-inclusive, so you pay one price up front and all your game drives, meals, and drinks are included.

Some TRAVEL THERAPY favorite picks for affordable safaris include:

- Djuma Game Reserve—Vuyatela Camp: www.djuma.co.za
- Rhino Walking Safaris: www.rws.co.za
- Honeyguide Tented Safari Camps: www.honeyguidecamp.com

If money isn't a factor, then you'll want to check out these over-the-top safari splurges, featuring the best of the best that the Kruger National Park has to offer.

- Singita Game Reserves: www.singita.com

- Sabi Sabi Private Game Reserve: www.sabisabi.com
- MalaMala Game Reserve: www.malamala.com
- Royal Malewane: www.royalmalewane.com

For help in picking the right safari camp, you can't go wrong working with the folks at Siyabona Africa Travel (www.siyabona.com) because this group specializes in South Africa safaris and there are no booking fees. These safari experts can often out-best the best deals on the Internet because they're in daily contact with the different safari camps. So even if you do your own research, check with Siyabona as well and see what magic they can work.

The South Africa Tourism site (www.southafrica.net) is also packed with helpful information, covering everything you need to know about getting to South Africa and enjoying yourself once you arrive.

The goal of any safari vacation is to spot the Big Five: the lion, leopard, elephant, rhino, and buffalo. Be sure to bring binoculars and have your best camera gear ready because what you'll see will blow you away. The whole time I was there I felt like I was living a fantasy. The colors, sites, and smells were like nothing I'd ever experienced.

The Kruger National Park more than lived up to my safari dreams. It's a powerful feeling to set a travel goal and obtain it, especially when the odds are stacked high against it. Going on the TRAVEL THERAPY trip you've

always dreamed of gives you the confidence you need to venture to even more challenging destinations. It makes you realize that anything is possible if you want it enough and are willing to work for it.

That's what TRAVEL THERAPY is all about—knowing that nothing in your life is unobtainable as long as you have the right attitude, drive, and determination. The world is waiting for you, so what are you waiting for?

Just Do It! Vacation Checklist

CHOOSE TRIPS WHERE YOU CAN:

- Take your time
- Explore new places
- Say you *finally* did it
- Enjoy the moment
- Fulfill a dream
- Take pride in your journey
- Live like you deserve to

▲ *Traveling off the Beaten Path, Rhino Post Safari Camp, South Africa*
© KAREN SCHALER

"With TRAVEL THERAPY, you can change your attitude by changing your environment."

—KAREN SCHALER

Chapter 11

Your Turn!

So where do you want to go? What is your travel dream? In the space that follows, write down your Travel Therapy choice. Putting down what you want on paper will bring you one step closer to turning your travel dream into a trip.

My TRAVEL THERAPY choice: _____

When I want to go: _____

Why I want to go: _____

_____

_____

_____

_____

_____

I would love to hear about your travel experience and how it changed your life. Just send me an email at kschaler@traveltherapytrips.com. To continue your Travel Therapy just log on to www.traveltherapytrips.com for daily updates on the most inspiring new travel trends and destinations. I'll see you on the next journey! Safe travels.

◄ *Peter Island, British Virgin Islands*
© KAREN SCHALER

TRAVEL THERAPY TOOLS

Heartbreak Hotel

Daring Destinations

SHARK DIVER
www.sharkdiver.com

SAN DIEGO SHARK DIVING
EXPEDITION
www.sdsharkdiving.com

TORREY PINES GLIDERPORT
www.flytorrey.com

SKIP BARBER RACING SCHOOL
www.skipbarber.com

HOMESTEAD-MIAMI RACING
SCHOOL
www.miamiracingschool.com

DALE JARRETT RACING
ADVENTURE
www.racingadventure.com

RICHARD PETTY DRIVING
EXPERIENCE
www.1800bepetty.com

JEFF GORDON RACING SCHOOL
www.andrettigordon.com

MARIO ANDRETTI RACING SCHOOL
www.andrettigordon.com

Action Adventures

ACAMPA NATURE ADVENTURES
www.acampapr.com

JAGUAR PAW JUNGLE RESORT
www.jaguarpaw.com

SUN VALLEY/KETCHUM CHAMBER
AND VISITORS BUREAU
www.visitsunvalley.com

Soothing Spa Escapes

GREATER PHOENIX CONVENTION
AND VISITORS BUREAU
www.visitphoenix.com

SCOTTSDALE CONVENTION
AND VISITORS BUREAU
www.scottsdalecvb.com

ROYAL PALMS RESORT AND SPA
www.royalpalmshotel.com

CENTRE FOR WELL-BEING—
THE PHOENICIAN
www.thephoenician.com

FOUR SEASONS SPA—THE FOUR
SEASONS AT TROON NORTH
www.fourseasons.com
/scottsdale

SPA AVANIA—HYATT REGENCY
SCOTTSDALE AT GAINEY RANCH
www.spaavania.com

REVIVE SPA—JW MARRIOT
DESERT RIDGE RESORT & SPA
www.jwdesertridgeresort.com

AGAVE SPA—THE WESTIN
KIERLAND RESORT & SPA
www.kierlandresort.com

WILLOW STREAM SPA—THE
FAIRMONT SCOTTSDALE PRINCESS
www.fairmont.com/scottsdale

THE BELLAGIO
www.bellagio.com

THEHOTEL
www.mandalaybay.com

THE VENETIAN
www.thevenetian.com

Qua Baths & Spa at Caesars Palace

QUA BATHS & SPA AT
CAESARS PALACE
www.caesarspalace.com

LE MERIGOT HOTEL AND SPA
www.lemerigothotel.com

SHUTTERS ON THE BEACH
www.shuttersonthebeach.com

WILLOW SPA
www.willowspa.com

The Big Chill

Water Retreats

GREAT BARRIER REEF
VISITORS BUREAU
www.great-barrier-reef.com

BEYOND THE REEF
www.diveyap.com

VISITORS CENTER OF THE
FEDERATED STATES OF
MICRONESIA
www.visit-fsm.org

Private Island Escapes

DESROCHES ISLAND RESORT
www.slh.com

BRITISH VIRGIN ISLANDS
www.bvitourism.com

Peaceful Playgrounds

FLORIDA KEYS TOURISM COUNCIL
www.fla-keys.com

HAWKS CAY RESORT
www.hawkscay.com

STEVE & DORIS COLGATE'S
OFFSHORE SAILING SCHOOL
www.offshore-sailing.com

THE NANTUCKET VISITORS
SERVICE
www.nantucket-ma.gov

CABANAS COPAL
www.cabanascopal.com

ZAHRA
www.zahra.com.mx

AZULIK
www.azulik.com

SARDINIA
www.sardinia.net
www.discover-sardinia.com

Ready For Romance

Romantic Destinations

MAROMA HOTEL
www.maromahotel.com

TIDES RESORT
www.tidesrivieramaya.com

PANGKOR LAUT RESORT
www.pangkorlautresort.com

Sailing Adventures

OFFSHORE SAILING SCHOOL
www.offshore-sailing.com

THE GRENADINES
www.grenadines.net

Quick Weekend Escapes

ONE&ONLY PALMILLA
www.oneandonlypalmilla.com

LAS VENTANAS AL PARAISO
www.lasventanas.com

LOS CABOS TOURISM BOARD
www.visitloscabos.org

BERMUDA DEPARTMENT OF
TOURISM
www.bermudatourism.com

THE MOORINGS
www.moorings.com

BRITISH VIRGIN ISLANDS
www.britishvirginislands.com

Pay It Forward

Construction Volunteer Projects

HABITAT FOR HUMANITY
www.habitat.org

AMBASSADORS FOR CHILDREN
www.ambassadorsfor
children.org

THAT'S MY SEAT! Sidebar

SEAT GURU
www.seatguru.com

Volunteering with Children

GOABROAD.COM
www.goabroad.com

I-TO-I
www.i-to-i.com

Going Green

GIBBON REHABILITATION PROJECT
www.gibbonproject.org

WILDERNESS VOLUNTEERS
www.wildernessvolunteers.org

PROWORLD SERVICE CORPS
www.myproworld.org

Reconnecting

Family-Friendly Vacations

LAKE TAHOE VISITORS BUREAU
www.visitinglaketahoe.com

NORTHSTAR RESORT
www.northstarattahoe.com

BANFF LAKE LOUISE TOURISM
www.banfflakelouise.com

ATLANTIS
www.atlantis.com

PARADISE ISLAND
www.nassauparadiseisland.com

Camping Adventures

WASHINGTON STATE TOURISM
www.experiencewa.com

NATIONAL PARK SERVICE
www.nps.gov

GRAND CANYON CHAMBER
& VISITOR'S BUREAU
www.grandcanyonvisitorbureau
.com

Escape for Couples

MONACO
www.monaco-consulate.com
www.visitmonaco.com

SONOMA COUNTY TOURISM
BUREAU
www.sonomacounty.com

MATAMANOA
www.matamanoa.com

Author's Pick

TY GURNEY SURF SCHOOL
www.tygurneysurfschool.com

OAHU VISITORS BUREAU
www.visit-oahu.com

Doctor's Orders

Best Beaches

CLUB MED
www.clubmed.us

GRACE BAY CLUB
www.gracebayclub.com

REGENT PALMS
www.regenthotels.com
/thepalms

TURKS AND CAICOS TOURIST
BOARD
www.turksandcaicos
tourism.com

SANTA MONICA CONVENTION
AND VISITORS BUREAU
www.santamonica.com

BVI TOURISM
www.bvitourism.com

Spa Vacations

MII AMO SPA
www.miiamo.com

SEDONA CHAMBER OF COMMERCE
www.visitsedona.com

LA QUINTA RESORT & CLUB
www.laquintaresort.com

VICEROY PALM SPRINGS
www.viceroypalmsprings.com

PALM SPRINGS BUREAU OF
TOURISM
www.palm-springs.org

MAUI VISITORS BUREAU
www.visitmaui.com

Vacation Home Rentals

VACATION RENTALS
www.vacationrentals.com

HAMPTONS VISITORS COUNCIL
www.hamptonsvisitors
council.com

THE HAMPTONS
www.hamptonstravelguide.com

CRYSTAL COAST TOURISM
www.crystalcoastnc.org

EMERALD ISLE
www.emeraldislerealty.com

MALIBU CHAMBER OF COMMERCE
www.malibu.org

CITY OF MALIBU
www.ci.malibu.ca.us

JUMBY BAY RESORT
www.jumbybayresort.com
www.jumbybayblog.com

Celebrate

Babymoon Vacations

BABYMOON RESOURCES
www.babymoonguide.com
www.babymoonfinder.com
www.spafinder.com

SCOTTSDALE CONVENTION AND
VISITORS BUREAU
www.scottsdalecvb.com

GREATER PHOENIX CONVENTION
AND VISITORS BUREAU
www.visitphoenix.com

HAWAII—THE BIG ISLAND
www.gohawaii.com

THE RITZ-CARLTON
www.ritzcarlton.com

FLORIDA COAST
www.visitflorida.com

Girlfriend Getaways

DISCOUNT BROADWAY SITES
www.broadwaybox.com
www.playbill.com
www.theatermania.com

NEW YORK PALACE HOTEL
www.newyorkpalace.com

EMPIRE HOTEL
www.empirehotelnyc.com

FOUR SEASONS HOTEL
NEW YORK CITY
www.fourseasons.com/
newyorkfs

EURAIL
www.eurail.com

EUROPE
www.visiteurope.com

FRENCH TOURIST OFFICE
www.francetourism.com

PARIS CONVENTION AND
VISITORS BUREAU
http://en.parisinfo.com

Romantic Escapes

MYSTIQUE
www.mystique.gr

PERIVOLAS
www.perivolas.gr

CANAVES OIA HOTEL
www.slh.com/canaves

VILLA KATIKIES
www.katikies.com/santorini-villas

KIRINI HOTEL
www.kirini.com

SANTORINI
www.santorinigreece.net
www.santoriniluxuryhotels.com

ROSEWOOD LITTLE DIX BAY
www.littledixbay.com

BIRAS CREEK
www.biras.com

TAHITI
www.tahiti-tourisme.com

BORA BORA
www.boraboraisland.com

THE FOUR SEASONS RESORT BORA BORA
www.fourseasons.com/borabora

BORA BORA LAGOON RESORT & SPA
www.boraboralagoon.com

LE MERIDIEN BORA BORA
www.starwoodhotels.com/lemeridien

HOTEL BORA BORA
www.amanresorts.com/hotelborabora

THE ST. REGIS BORA BORA RESORT
www.starwoodhotels.com/stregis

SOFITEL BORA BORA MOTU
www.sofitel.com

BALEARIC ISLANDS
www.illesbalears.es

Lost and Found

Unique Group Tours

DENMARK TOURIST BUREAU
www.visitdenmark.com

WAYFARERS
www.thewayfarers.com

NOMADIC EXPEDITIONS
www.nomadicexpeditions.com

MONGOLIA TOURISM
www.mongoliatourism.gov.mn

Cruises

CRUISE LINE INTERNATIONAL ASSOCIATION
www.cruising.org

TRAVEL ALASKA
www.travelalaska.com

GREEK TOURISM
www.greek-tourism.gr

MEXICO TOURISM BOARD
www.visitmexico.com

REGENT SEVEN SEAS CRUISES
www.rssc.com

PRINCESS CRUISES
www.princess.com

CELEBRITY CRUISES
www.celebritycruises.com

CRUISE WEST
www.cruisewest.com

CARNIVAL
www.carnival.com

ROYAL CARIBBEAN INTERNATIONAL
www.royalcaribbean.com

HOLLAND AMERICA LINE
www.hollandamerica.com

NORWEGIAN CRUISE LINE
www.ncl.com

SEABOURN CRUISES
www.seabourn.com

SILVERSEA
www.silversea.com

CRYSTAL CRUISES
www.crystalcruises.com

ORIENT LINES
www.orientlines.com

COSTA CRUISES
www.costacruises.com

WINDSTAR CRUISES
www.windstarcruises.com

OCEANIA CRUISES
www.oceaniacruises.com

All-Inclusive Vacations

DOMINICAN REPUBLIC
www.godominicanrepublic.com

THE BUNGALOWS
www.thebungalows.com

ROYAL HIDEAWAY
www.royalhideaway.com

MEXICO TOURISM BOARD
www.visitmexico.com

PLAYACAR
www.playacarallinclusive.com

CURTAIN BLUFF
www.curtainbluff.com

ANTIGUA AND BARBUDA
DEPARTMENT OF TOURISM
www.antigua-barbuda.org

JUMBY BAY RESORT
www.jumbybayresort.com

Author's Pick

DACHUA, GERMANY
www.kz-gedenkstaette
-dachau.de

Reinvent

Unique Destinations

DUBAI DEPARTMENT OF TOURISM
AND COMMERCE MARKETING
www.dubaitourism.ae

SAFARI BEACH LODGE
www.safaribeachlodge.net

CLUB MAKOKOLA
www.clubmak.com

NTCHISI FOREST LODGE
www.ntchisi.com

MALAWI
http://malawi.safari.co.za

MALAWI TOURISM
www.malawitourism.com

CENTER FOR DISEASE CONTROL
AND PREVENTION
www.cdc.gov

VIETNAM NATIONAL
ADMINISTRATION OF TOURISM
www.vietnamtourism.com

U.S. DEPARTMENT OF STATE
www.state.gov

Solo Travel

TIDES ZIHUATANEJO
www.tideszihuatanejo.com

MEXICO TOURISM BOARD
www.visitmexico.com

YOUTH HOSTELS ASSOCIATION
OF NEW ZEALAND
www.yha.co.nz

TOURISM NEW ZEALAND
www.newzealand.com

ITALIAN GOVERNMENT
TOURIST BOARD
www.italiantourism.com

ITALIAN COOKING SCHOOLS
www.it-schools.com
www.italiancookerycourse.com
www.villagiona.it
www.absoluteitalia.com
www.cucinaconvista.it
www.villasanmichele.com

MONTANA DUDE RANCHES
www.dryheadranch.com
www.sweetgrassranch.com
www.triplecreekranch.com

An Old Dog Can Learn New Tricks!

VALRHONA
www.valrhona.com

ECOLE CHOCOLAT
www.ecolechocolat.com

RHONE-ALPES TOURISM
www.rhonealpes-tourism.co.uk

AUTHOR'S PICK
APARTHEID MUSEUM
www.apartheidmuseum.org

THE SAXON BOUTIQUE HOTEL
AND SPA
www.saxon.co.za

THE ELLERMAN HOUSE
www.ellermanhouse.com

THE EZARD HOUSE
www.ezardhouse.com

MOUNT NELSON HOTEL
www.mountnelson.co.za

HOUT BAY MANOR
www.houtbaymanor.co.za

VINEYARD HOTEL & SPA
www.vineyard.co.za

DADDY LONG LEGS HOTEL
www.daddylonglegs.co.za

SOUTH AFRICA TOURISM
www.southafrica.net

Just Do It!

Golf Vacations

SCOTLAND'S NATIONAL TOURISM
ORGANIZATION
www.visitscotland.com

ST. ANDREWS
www.standrews.org.uk

ROYAL TROON GOLF CLUB
www.royaltroon.co.uk

PRESTWICK GOLF CLUB
www.prestwickgc.co.uk